MONEY

ADDICTION

LIVING IN A
DOPAMINE ECONOMY

by

F. M. ROTH

CONTENTS

INTRODUCTION

You won't like everything you read in this book. But you're not here for comfort. You're here for the truth. You think you have money. But money has you. That's not drama. That's diagnosis.

It controls your time. It steers your choices. It defines your worth. You wake up with it in mind. You go to sleep with it on your chest.

It tells you who to admire. Who to envy. Who to become. It promises freedom—then chains your soul to a number on a screen.

This book is not about how to save better or invest smarter. This is not another feel-good guide to attract wealth with positive thinking.

There's no budgeting chart here. No financial hacks. Because you don't need another strategy. You need liberation.

We've turned money into something it was never meant to be: a drug. A psychological stimulant. A hit of safety.

A high of validation. You crave it. Fear losing it. Hate needing it. It's no longer just a tool. It's the air your ego breathes.

But it didn't start with you. You were programmed—by systems, schools, parents, screens. You were told that value comes with a price tag.

That security means submission. That a six-figure salary is the ticket to self-worth.

And you believed it. We all did. This book is here to break that spell.

It will shake your illusions, expose your fears, and pull the plug on your dependency. You may get angry. You may deny it. You may even want to stop reading.

That's okay. Withdrawal is never easy.

But if you're still here by the last page, something inside you will have shifted.

CHAPTER ONE

THE BEGINNING OF THE HIGH

"You didn't fall in love with money - you got high on the feeling it faked."

THE FIRST HIT

There's a reason you feel that unease when you check your bank balance. That jolt in your chest, that tightness in your jaw when an unexpected expense shows up. That electric pulse when money enters your account, and the crash when it leaves. That's not just financial management. That's chemical. Emotional. Psychological. It's the tremor of your nervous system reacting to something we've long stopped recognizing as dangerous—because it's everywhere. It rewards you. It punishes you. It triggers anxiety, relief, elation, guilt. That's not how a tool behaves. That's how a drug behaves.

Once upon a time, money didn't exist. And yet, people lived. They hunted, they gathered, they bartered. Communities relied on each other for survival, not because they were idealistic, but because there was no other choice. A loaf of bread was traded for firewood. A handmade cloak might be exchanged for meat. It was simple and transparent. Every trade required you to look someone in the eye. You knew what you were giving. You understood what you were receiving. There was no illusion, no value floating in the air, no manipulation embedded in the process.

But that system had limits. Bartering only works when needs align. It collapses when someone has nothing you want. So humans created something new—**a placeholder for value**. Metal stamped into coins. Cowry shells. Salt. Beads. Eventually, paper marked with the signatures of kings. The abstraction was brilliant. With money, you didn't need mutual need—you just needed belief. Belief that this thing, this token, was worth something because everyone else believed it too.

And belief… is powerful. It's the raw material of every addiction. The moment enough people agree something has value, it becomes real—not just economically, but emotionally. And that's where the trouble began.

We weren't prepared for what money could do to our minds. What began as a tool of convenience slowly morphed into something else. At first, it brought security. A handful of coins could guarantee food. A pouch of silver meant safety from hunger. But then it started to buy more than necessities. It bought admiration. It bought control. It bought distance from discomfort. And as money began to promise more than survival, it also began to change us.

This was the **first high**. The moment when acquiring money didn't just fill your stomach—it filled your ego. It filled the silence. It soothed the fear. It gave you the illusion that you mattered more. That you were seen. That you were rising. And once people felt that—once they felt that rush—they needed more of it. Not to live. But to feel alive.

This wasn't greed. That's too shallow a word. This was emotional dependence. This was survival, rewired. We began to confuse money with meaning. The man with more coins wasn't just richer. He was better. He was smarter, more capable, more deserving. We started assigning value to human beings using the very thing we had created to make life easier. The servant who cleaned, who stitched, who toiled? Worth less. The man who owned land, who counted coins, who gave orders? Worth more. The chain was invisible, but it held tight.

And so we began to measure life itself through currency. Every dream came with a price tag. Every decision—whether to marry, to study, to move, to stay—was filtered through the lens of cost. We stopped asking, "What do I want?" and started asking, "What can I afford?" Money wasn't just guiding the economy—it was taking the wheel of our choices, our identities, and our worth.

No one noticed how sick we were becoming because the symptoms were praised. The more you worked, the more you were applauded. The more you hoarded, the more respected you became. Frugality, ambition, hustle—they all wore the mask of virtue. And behind that mask, the addiction deepened.

We built temples to money—banks, stock markets, shopping malls. We created rituals around it—paydays, sales, investments. We made it sacred, untouchable. We stopped questioning its morality because we feared its absence more than we feared its control.

And all the while, we told ourselves we were advancing. Modernizing. Evolving. But in truth, we were sedating. Our emotional vocabulary began to shrink. Joy became a transaction. Love became a luxury. Identity became a brand. Everything that once made us human was being rewritten by a number. And the more we believed in it, the less we remembered how to live without it.

We are generations into this high now. Children learn to count with toy money before they learn to count their emotions. Teenagers are told to choose careers not by passion, but by "financial stability." Adults drown in debt chasing a life they were told would make them happy—only to find themselves emptier with every purchase.

That's what addiction does. It lies. It promises pleasure, then delivers dependence. It tells you you're in control while it rewires your brain to beg for more. The worst part? It feels normal. Because everyone around you is high, too.

But this wasn't always normal. And it doesn't have to stay this way.

Understanding the first hit is the beginning of seeing clearly. Of waking up. Because the truth is: you weren't born to be a customer. You weren't born to be a paycheck. You weren't meant to calculate your life in interest rates, taxes, and credit scores. You were meant to be whole, even without a wallet.

The next time you feel the rush from a paycheck, or the anxiety from an unexpected bill, pause. Not to judge yourself—but to observe. That sensation in your gut? That pressure in your chest? That's the residue of centuries of belief. It's not personal. It's systemic. But now, you can see it.

And once you see it, you can't unsee it.

You can begin to ask the questions that matter. Who taught me that money equals worth? When did I start equating success with numbers? What would I choose if fear and cost weren't part of the equation?

Because money was meant to serve you. Not sedate you.

This was the beginning of the high. The first taste of emotional control disguised as economic evolution. And if we can trace where it started, we just might begin to understand how to break free.

THE RISE OF EMOTIONAL CURRENCY

Money didn't need to be real to have power. It only needed to be believed. And once belief set in—deep, unquestioned belief—it evolved into something far more potent than a tool of trade. It became an extension of self. A mirror of worth. A silent dictator embedded in every decision we made. That was the rise of emotional currency. It wasn't about buying things anymore. It was about buying meaning.

Let's be clear: emotional currency doesn't live in your wallet. It lives in your nervous system. In that jolt of pride when you swipe your platinum card. In the flash of shame when you count change. In the instant jealousy you feel seeing someone post their luxury vacation while you heat leftovers. It lives in comparisons. In the subtle nods of approval when someone says, "They're doing well." In the invisible scorecard we carry in our heads, measuring ourselves against the cars parked outside, the clothes on backs, the size of homes. Emotional currency is the invisible economy of **worth**, and it is fueled by perception, not reality.

We were never warned about this shift. No one sat us down to say, "One day, money will decide how lovable you feel." But it happened. Somewhere between being told to get good grades to land a good job, and watching our parents sigh over bills, we learned the real lesson: money is emotion. Money is love, safety, pride, envy, respect, power—all wrapped in numbers and dressed as logic.

And society rewarded this shift. Wealth wasn't just admired—it was spiritualized. In ancient cultures, kings and emperors weren't just rulers; they were considered gods on earth. Why? Because they had gold. They had land. They had the visible markers of abundance. Wealth became divine. Poverty became punishment. And slowly, the morality of the world bent around this illusion. Being poor wasn't just a lack of resources—it was seen as a failure of character.

Look at ancient Egypt. Pharaohs were buried with riches, with the belief that wealth would accompany them into the afterlife. Look at Rome. Senators measured their success in coin, not virtue. In early Asian empires, merchants gained prestige not because of what they created, but because of what they collected. And in every corner of history, wherever emotional currency emerged, human value started shrinking into ledgers.

You feel it today, don't you?

When someone says, "He's successful," they're not talking about kindness. They're talking about income. When someone says, "She married well," they mean financially. When people say, "I'm behind in life," they're talking about money. Not wisdom. Not inner peace. Just dollars, digits, and debt.

This is not a coincidence. This is conditioning.

Money hijacked the human experience. It crawled into our most sacred spaces—our relationships, our identities, our sense of belonging—and rewrote the code. It taught us that giving isn't generosity unless it comes with cost. That accomplishments aren't real unless they're profitable. That dreams aren't valid unless they can be monetized. It took our intangible beauty—our creativity, our courage, our spirit—and asked: "Can this be sold?"

The answer, increasingly, became yes. Art was no longer for expression. It became a brand. Love was no longer about connection. It became a contract. Careers stopped being callings and became survival strategies. Emotional currency had infected everything. We didn't fall in love—we assessed financial compatibility. We didn't pursue purpose—we calculated ROI.

Even our emotions became transactional. Pride came from raises. Joy came from purchases. Relief came from payments. Anxiety came from bills. Our emotional range was narrowed to numbers. And no one questioned it, because everyone was doing it. Everyone was chasing more.

We dress it up with pretty phrases—"financial freedom," "abundant mindset," "making smart money moves"—but the root is the same: we're still trying to feel something deeper through something external. We want to feel **enough**. And money promised to deliver that feeling. It whispered, "If you just make more…… they'll respect you. You'll be safe. You'll finally rest."

But money is a moving target. And emotional currency is an endless loop.

You get the raise. The moment feels good. Then it fades. You upgrade the car. The compliments come. Then they stop. You buy the house. You host the party. You post the photo. The likes come. Then what? The crash. The void. The sudden panic that maybe, just maybe, this wasn't fulfillment. Maybe this was just another **hit**.

That's why it feels like a high. Because it is. Neurologically, emotionally, spiritually—it's designed to stimulate, reward, and then leave you wanting more. The dopamine rush of a deposit. The thrill of a purchase. The ego boost of admiration. But like any drug, it fades. And you're left chasing the next one. Bigger. Shinier. Louder. More.

And when you can't get the high? That's when shame sets in.

Shame is the shadow of emotional currency. It tells you you're not trying hard enough. That you're lazy. That you're behind. That you're failing. It wraps around your mind and squeezes until you start believing you deserve less—because you earn less. And suddenly, it's not just about having money. It's about being worthy of it.

This is how society keeps the addiction running. Through emotional blackmail. Through unspoken rules that say: If you don't have money, you're less of a man. Less of a woman. Less of a parent. Less of a human being. It is psychological violence, dressed in the clean language of finance.

We call it "responsibility." But what it really is…… is fear. Fear of judgment. Fear of invisibility. Fear of not being **enough** in a world that only sees numbers.

So we perform. We overwork. We overspend. We overextend. We smile through the burnout. We polish the Instagram version of ourselves while silently breaking inside. And we convince ourselves it's normal. That this is adulthood. That this is maturity.

But that's the lie emotional currency tells you: That you're only as good as what you can earn. That your value is negotiable.

That your existence must be justified with productivity. You weren't born with that belief. You were taught it. Programmed with it. Raised in it.

And now, it's time to see it for what it is.

Because emotional currency is not your truth. It's a glitch in the code. A virus in the mind. You were not meant to price your peace. You were not meant to lease your joy. You were not meant to auction off your identity for applause.

You were born whole. Valuable. Without terms and conditions. But somewhere along the way, they sold you the lie that money completes you. And you bought it.

But here's the radical truth: You can stop. You can unsubscribe. You can opt out of this emotional economy and decide, finally, to feel enough—without a purchase receipt to prove it.

"You were taught to call it success. But it's just the prettiest form of obedience."

THE DOPAMINE ECONOMY

Money is not just something you use. It's something you feel. That tight sensation in your chest when your card declines, the rush of excitement when your salary hits your account, the urge to check your bank balance even though you just checked it thirty minutes ago—these aren't just habits. They're reactions. Biological, emotional, and neurological. They come from a part of your brain designed to keep you alive but now hijacked by a man-made invention: currency. The system may be financial, but the addiction is chemical.

Let's stop pretending this is purely rational. It's not. There's a very real, measurable change in your brain when you anticipate or receive money. Scientists have studied this. Functional MRIs show that the brain lights up in the same areas when people expect to win money as it does when addicts anticipate their next drug hit. Specifically, the nucleus accumbens—the pleasure center—is triggered not by possession, but by expectation. That means it's not even the money that hooks you. It's the idea of it. The anticipation. The fantasy. The hit before the hit.

This is the dopamine economy. A system that rewards the mere thought of gain, not necessarily the gain itself. It's why people feel euphoric before payday but empty two days later. It's why shopping can feel like a celebration, even when you don't need anything. It's why checking your stocks or crypto portfolio can become an hourly habit. Your brain is chasing dopamine—the chemical that tells you something good is coming, even if it never arrives. We're not addicted to money itself. We're addicted to how it makes us feel for a fleeting moment.

The cycle is so normalized that no one questions it. Wake up. Work. Get paid. Spend. Repeat. But what's really happening under the surface? Each step is tied to a neurochemical response. When the paycheck hits, you feel relief. When you make a purchase, there's a spike of excitement. When you get approval for a loan, there's pride. But when your account dips too low, panic kicks in. Cortisol floods your body. You're not making decisions—you're reacting to waves of pleasure and fear, manipulated by numbers on a screen.

What makes this dangerous is that it doesn't feel dangerous. In fact, it's praised. Hustle culture encourages you to chase higher income, climb faster, never stop moving. You're admired for working 14-hour days and pushing past burnout, but no one asks why you're doing it. No one wants to admit that most of us aren't chasing purpose—we're chasing a feeling. A fix. The next spike. Like any drug, the high fades fast, and the comedown leaves us restless, anxious, and hollow. But instead of detoxing, we convince ourselves we need more. More money. More status. More proof that we're okay.

You might think addiction is reserved for extreme cases—substances, gambling, risky behavior. But addiction is any repetitive behavior that brings short-term relief and long-term harm, especially when it becomes compulsive. By that definition, how many of us are already addicted to the financial hit? How many of us define a good day by how much we made or lost? How many times do we check our bank balance—not because we need to—but because we're chasing reassurance?

This explains why financial stress can be so deeply traumatic. It's not just about lack—it's about withdrawal. When money is low, we don't just feel insecure. We feel physically and emotionally threatened. Our bodies respond with tension, headaches, anxiety, sleeplessness. Not because we're shallow. But because our entire sense of control and identity has been chemically tethered to financial status. When the money disappears, the emotional safety net vanishes with it. It's not about dollars—it's about regulation. Peace. Belonging. Power. These are emotional needs. And somewhere along the line, we wired them all into one outlet: money.

The worst part is how quiet this addiction is. It doesn't scream like alcohol. It doesn't leave track marks like heroin. It looks like success. It smells like progress. It hides behind paychecks and portfolios. And because it's reinforced by culture, it's almost impossible to spot. You're praised for working overtime, admired for hitting financial milestones, envied for your lifestyle. No one sees the sleepless nights. The guilt. The emptiness after the purchase. The sense of "is this it?" that creeps in after every new financial achievement.

When people say they want financial freedom, they usually mean freedom from this feeling. Freedom from the tight grip of worry, from the constant calculation, from the noise that money creates in the back of their minds. But money can't free you from a pattern it created. It can't undo the wiring. That's your job. And the first step is awareness. To notice the hit. To see the craving. To pause and ask yourself, "Is this real security—or just the illusion of it?"

It's not about rejecting money. It's about reclaiming your mind from its grip. It's about learning how to feel stable, enough, and calm without needing a transaction to validate it. If you can't feel peace without checking your income, that's not wealth. That's dependency. If your self-worth rises and falls with your earnings, that's not empowerment. That's emotional captivity.

The dopamine economy doesn't want you to rest. It wants you on edge, hungry for more, convinced that the next raise, sale, or deal will finally bring you satisfaction. It won't. Not until you rewire what satisfaction even means. True freedom isn't more money. It's the ability to live well when the money is silent.

This is your brain on money. Not just spending. Not just earning. But cycling—through hope, reward, crash, and craving. And until you name the pattern, it owns you.

You were not designed to be a profit machine. You were not meant to measure your life by deposits and debits. You are more than your net worth. But you'll never feel that truth if you keep letting your brain chase chemicals instead of clarity.

CURRENCY AND CONTROL

Money may have started as a tool, but those who understood its emotional power knew it could be weaponized. Once humanity believed in currency, it didn't take long before institutions emerged to control it. Kings minted coins with their faces, not for vanity, but to remind people: your value comes from me. Banks held gold and printed paper, not to make trade easier, but to make sure you needed them. Governments collected taxes, not just to run nations, but to tether your work, your time, and your survival to a system that could never be exited without consequence.

Money became a leash. Wrapped in laws, signed with policy, backed by force. What once made you free to exchange became the very thing you were now forced to use. And it was designed that way. Control doesn't require violence when you can engineer dependence. And that's exactly what the system did.

You don't question money because it's been baked into every structure that touches your life. Your education taught you how to earn it. Your job trained you to chase it. Your government tracks it. Your worth in society—your house, your healthcare, your status—is calculated through it. They don't have to control you directly. They just have to control what you need.

That's how control works best—not through chains, but through belief. If you believe you need the system, then you'll never rebel. You'll never walk away. You'll call it "adulthood." You'll call it "being responsible." You'll call it "growing up." And you'll teach your children the same thing, thinking it's wisdom.

But how much of your life is truly yours when every hour of your day is monetized? When every decision is filtered through affordability? When your dreams come second to your bills? That's not sovereignty. That's ownership—just not the kind you think.

People say "money is power." But the truth is darker. Money is a proxy for control. And those who understand this don't just chase wealth—they manufacture the belief systems that keep everyone else chasing it too.

SOCIETY'S FIRST ADDICTS

When the first few realized how money changed perception, they understood something dangerous: they didn't need to be valuable —they just needed to look like they were. This was the birth of class. The moment human beings were sorted not by wisdom, strength, or kindness, but by appearance—by the illusion of abundance. It wasn't enough to have enough. You had to have more than someone else.

Class isn't natural. It's manufactured. The creation of elites required an underclass. You can't feel superior unless someone is beneath you. And money became the easiest weapon to divide the masses. Once emotional value became linked to wealth, society didn't just reward the rich—it internalized the inferiority of the poor.

This was the rise of greed—not as a flaw, but as a virtue. The more you amassed, the more you were admired. The more you took, the more power you had. Compassion became secondary. Efficiency, competition, domination—these became the new gods.

But what no one saw coming was the spread of the addiction. It didn't stay at the top. It trickled down. Everyone started chasing the image. The clothes. The car. The neighborhood. Not for function, but for meaning. Because we were told that's how you matter.

Greed became invisible because it wore the face of ambition. But the line between desire and destruction blurred a long time ago. When your sense of worth rises from comparison, you will always crave more than you need—and resent those who have more than you.

Every time you said 'I can't afford that,' what you really meant was, 'I don't own my time.'

THE LOSS OF SIMPLICITY

Once, long ago, people were content with enough. Food on the table. Shelter. Community. Purpose. These were enough. And they still are. But we don't believe it anymore. Not because the truth changed—but because marketing rewrote it.

You live in a culture that profits from your dissatisfaction. If you feel whole, you won't spend. If you feel worthy, you won't chase. So the machine must convince you—day after day—that you're lacking. That you're late. That you're small. That you're behind. And every product, every service, every upgrade is positioned as the fix to a problem you didn't even know you had.

This is why enough is dangerous to the system. Because "enough" doesn't scale. You can't build empires off of contentment. So the economy must stay hungry. It must create restlessness. It must whisper in your ear every morning: more. More clients. More savings. More growth. More goals.

You've been sold the idea that growth is good—always. That scaling is success. But nature doesn't grow endlessly. Trees stop growing. Bodies mature. Healthy ecosystems balance. Only tumors grow without end. And maybe what we've built isn't an economy—it's a pathology.

Simplicity isn't failure. It's freedom. But you'll never feel that freedom if your nervous system only relaxes at the sight of a balance sheet.

You don't fear being broke. You fear being invisible in a world that worships wealth.

THE BEGINNING OF DEPENDENCE

This is where it all comes together. This is the moment money stopped being a means to an end and became your self. You stopped saying, "I have money" and started saying, "I am successful." The job title became the identity. The salary became the personality. The lifestyle became the performance.

This shift wasn't accidental. The economy isn't just external—it's internalized. The financial system moved from spreadsheets into your sense of self. And now, most people can't even separate their value from their income. When they earn less, they feel less. When they lose money, they lose confidence. When they go broke, they lose identity.

But what is identity if it's built on something so unstable?

How can you build a life on something that changes daily? How can you define your worth with a number that the system invented, manipulated, and owns?

This is the dependence that runs deeper than bills. This is the quiet death of inner sovereignty. The moment you began seeing yourself as a bank account in a body.

And now, the only question that matters is this: Are you ready to remember who you were before the addiction?

Because if you don't detach from the identity the system gave you, you will never know who you really are. And they will keep selling you versions of yourself—until the real you disappears.

"You thought you were earning – it was your ego getting fed and your freedom getting sold."

REFLECTION QUESTIONS

- When did you first feel like money defined your worth?
- Have you ever made a major life choice out of fear of being financially unsafe?
- What would your life look like if you made decisions without factoring in money?
- Which emotion does money most trigger in you—fear, pride, shame, or power?
- Are you willing to consider that the life you're chasing might be a financial illusion?

CHAPTER TWO

CASHJUNKIES

"Everyone is addicted to money, but not everyone admits it."

THE EPIDEMIC OF WANT

You think you want more money. You think it's about the cars, the house, the gadgets, the vacations, the things that everyone tells you will make you happy. But deep down, it's not about the things at all. It's about filling the hole. It's about the belief that money can make you whole—that somehow, it will give you what you've always been missing.

This isn't just your problem. It's an epidemic. A disease that has spread through every layer of society, quietly infecting people of all walks of life. Money isn't just a means to live anymore. It's become the very reason we live.

When did the need for "stuff" become a need for self-worth? When did accumulating possessions become the ultimate form of success? The moment we accepted money as the measuring stick for everything, we gave away our power. We gave away our authenticity. And we gave away our ability to truly feel free.

Let's get something clear: this addiction isn't just about consumerism. It's about validation. Money is no longer about what you need. It's about what you're told you should need. It's about buying what you think will make you look a certain way, feel a certain way, be a certain way. Every purchase is a message to the world, to your friends, to your family—and to yourself—that you are worthy. But here's the thing: you never needed any of it to be worthy.

The need to have more, do more, and be more is the epidemic of modern society. It's no longer just about having enough to survive. It's about having enough to prove that you've made it. Because somewhere along the way, we stopped looking for happiness in relationships, in fulfillment, in purpose, and started seeking it in the wallet. The moment you believe that your worth is defined by your earnings is the moment you start to spiral into this money trap. The hole inside you can't be filled with more zeros in your bank account. But that's exactly what society tells you every day. It's the trap you don't even see until you're caught.

Think about it. You go to work every day. You chase promotions, you work overtime, you sell a part of yourself to meet deadlines and KPIs, not just for survival—but for the illusion of success. But what is success? Success, as defined by the money-driven world we've built, is about having more than others. Having the car, the house, the status. And because everyone is doing it, it seems normal. It's normal to feel incomplete unless you've bought into the idea that your value is tied to what you have, not who you are.

But the truth is much darker. The truth is that this addiction to money, this desire for more, is a distraction from what you're really running from. You're running from the truth that you don't believe you're enough. And when you don't feel enough, you fill the void with possessions, with the currency of the world. This is how society keeps you in the loop. The more you want, the more you need.

Every ad you see, every influencer's sponsored post, every bill you pay, is a reminder of this unspoken rule: You are not enough unless you have more. This epidemic isn't about money; it's about what money promises you. It promises freedom, it promises happiness, it promises acceptance, and it delivers none of these things. Money is the carrot that keeps you running, but the finish line keeps moving. And the farther you run, the less you feel you can ever catch up.

But it's even more sinister than that. It's not just the individuals trapped in the cycle. It's the collective, the entire society. The system is engineered to keep everyone chasing. Consumer culture doesn't just teach us to buy things—it teaches us to want things. And this epidemic has become so ingrained that it's hard to even know what wanting something without money attached would feel like.

From the moment you were born, you were conditioned into this cycle. The toys you were given, the brands you wore, the very idea that "more is better"—it was all part of the programming. Children today don't just play with toys—they play with brands. You don't just watch commercials—you internalize them. "I need this," "I deserve that," "If I don't have this, I'm not enough." The lie that society tells you is that want is normal. It's not. Wanting is the symptom of not being whole. And the more you want, the less you realize how much you've lost of who you really are.

The epidemic of want is not just a personal issue. It's a societal one. The culture around you creates this unending need for consumption and, by extension, this unending need for more money. Money becomes the answer to everything. If you're not chasing it, you're seen as lazy, irresponsible, and out of touch. People don't talk about being content with less. They talk about striving for more. It's a badge of honor to be overwhelmed with bills and overwork because the alternative—being "content" with less—is treated as failure.

We live in a world where happiness is commodified. We're told that happiness can be bought in the form of material goods, in the form of experiences that cost money, and in the form of lifestyles that require vast amounts of wealth. We're told that the more we own, the happier we will be, the more fulfilled we will feel. But that's a lie. A lie so pervasive, we've become blind to it.

This epidemic of want is so ingrained that it's considered aspiration. But what are we aspiring to? We're aspiring to a life built on debt, competition, and a hollow sense of self. The addiction to money isn't just about earning more, it's about constantly proving your worth to yourself and to others. It's about needing more, even when you already have enough. And even when you know that enough doesn't make you happy.

In fact, the more you buy, the more you spend, the more you try to satisfy this craving, the emptier you feel. You get the new car, the new shoes, the new tech, and for a moment, you feel good. You feel seen. But when the newness wears off—and it always does—you're left chasing the next purchase, the next fix. This is the hamster wheel you're on. This is the addiction that never lets you stop running.

It's not just an individual addiction. It's a cultural epidemic that keeps people from feeling enough in their own skin. This is why people feel so empty after they've bought everything they could possibly need. The hole isn't in their bank account. It's inside them. Money, the culture of consumption, promises to fill that void, but it can't. And that's the reality we all live in.

THE CURRENCY OF STATUS

There's a reason we treat the wealthy differently.

They don't just have money. They have power.

And that power? It doesn't just buy things. It buys respect, admiration, even admiration.

We live in a world where money is social capital—where what you own, what you can buy, and what you're seen spending tells others exactly who you are. And this is where the addiction begins to take its most insidious form. It's not enough to just have wealth. You need to show it. You need to project it. The moment money is no longer just about survival, but about status, we enter into a psychological and emotional labyrinth from which we rarely escape.

Money doesn't just buy possessions. It buys the illusion of value. The belief that because you have more of it, you matter more. Money becomes your ticket into exclusive circles, your access to power, your symbol of respectability. The rich don't just buy things—they curate themselves. They purchase not just luxury, but identity. And when society looks at them, they see it. They see the house, the car, the clothes—and they assume that they are the embodiment of success. But is that really success? Or is it just a performance?

This is the world we've built. A world where our social value is often measured in currency. If you don't believe this, just think about the last time you were at a party or social gathering, and someone started talking about their new job, their bonus, their salary. What was your first instinct? Did you feel happy for them or did you feel that twinge of jealousy? Did you start calculating your own worth by comparing your own financial status to theirs? Don't lie to yourself: we all do it.

It's not just you. This is what we're taught. This is the system we've been born into. We don't just measure people by what they do or who they are. We measure them by how much they have.

It's a game, and most people are playing it, whether they realize it or not. The wealthy are not simply rich. They are symbolically rich, symbolically powerful, and often, symbolically better than others. That's how society treats them, whether they want it or not. And it works. It works because we all want to be seen as better. The game is simple: the more you have, the more respect you command.

But what's worse than that, what's more insidious, is that society teaches you to internalize this value. Money isn't just a tool to buy things. It's a means of proving your worth to the world around you. This is why people compare. This is why we feel the need to keep up with the Joneses. This is why we act like we're successful when we're drowning in debt. We've been told the more you have, the more you are.

But it's a lie. It's the most dangerous lie ever told. It creates a class system based not on what we give, but on what we can afford to give. And it forces us to measure ourselves against other people's possessions, not their character.

Money is a social construct that has been invested with power. It's not just about the freedom it brings, or the opportunities it provides. It's about social proof. It's about telling the world, "I am someone of value. I am worthy." We see it everywhere. The brands you wear, the places you dine, the vehicles you drive—they are a reflection of how you want to be seen. And here's the kicker: the more you can be seen, the more respect you command. It's the currency of status.

Look at social media.

Look at Instagram, look at TikTok, look at Facebook. The lifestyle that's shown is a life of perfection. The images that get shared are of luxury, success, the perfect family, the perfect holiday. But do you ever stop and wonder how much of it is real? Do you ever stop and ask, "How much of this is performance?"

People don't post their struggles. They don't post their debts. They don't post their cracks. And we're all complicit in this. The wealthy post their curated lives. The middle class posts their "hustle" moments. And even the poor post their moments of glory, hiding the truth about their finances. Because in this society, you are only as good as the money you show the world.

So what happens when you buy into this lie?

You start to think that your worth, your value, is tied to how much money you make. You chase a life that isn't yours. You make decisions based on what you think will elevate your social capital. You go into debt to keep up appearances. You sacrifice time with your family to work longer hours and earn more. You spend money you don't have on things you don't need just to keep up with the Joneses.

This is where money begins to destroy your life. Because the more you try to show the world how rich you are, the poorer you become. And I'm not just talking about finances. I'm talking about your spirit, your mental health, your well-being. The more you sell your soul to the idea of being seen as successful, the more you lose yourself in the process.

Let's break this down.

People are consumed by the idea that money buys respect. That it buys validation. That it gives them status. But the truth is, respect doesn't come from what you show—it comes from who you are. True wealth isn't about what you have in your bank account. It's about what you have within. But no one tells you that. The system tells you to keep chasing. Keep pushing. Keep earning. And for what? To gain the world's approval? To live a life that others can envy? Is that really the prize? Is that really the endgame?

Because here's the thing: money doesn't make you better than anyone else. It doesn't make you more worthy. But in a world that glorifies wealth and materialism, it can certainly make you feel like you are. It's the ultimate illusion: the belief that who you are depends on how much you have.

This is the currency of status. This is the psychological trap that keeps us all chasing, never stopping, never feeling enough. We're all playing a game where the stakes are set by someone else's rules, and we're never told the game is rigged.

But it's time to wake up. It's time to ask yourself: What if I stopped buying into this illusion?

ADDICTION ON A MASS SCALE

We've been sold a lie. A lie that's so ingrained in the fabric of modern life that we don't even question it anymore.

The lie is this: More is better.

That's the slogan of consumerism. It's been drilled into our heads since the first TV commercial aired, since the first ad popped up on a newspaper, since the first shopping mall opened its doors. The message is clear: Buy. More. Consume. And you'll be happy.

But here's the truth that no one wants to admit: this isn't just marketing. This is addiction. The world isn't just selling us things. It's selling us a feeling. It's selling us the idea that we can fill the emptiness inside us with stuff. And the more we consume, the emptier we become.

It's a cycle that's designed to keep us wanting more, forever.

This is how the addiction works. And make no mistake: it's an addiction as real as any substance abuse.

At the heart of consumer culture is the promise of instant gratification. You don't have to wait for happiness, success, or satisfaction. You can buy it. That new pair of shoes? Instant boost of confidence. That shiny new phone? Instant relief from your social anxiety. That expensive vacation? Instant joy, until the pictures are posted.

The world feeds us these promises: if you buy this, you'll feel better. If you own that, you'll be complete. It doesn't matter that the happiness fades. It's always about the next purchase, the next "fix." And just like any other addiction, this cycle doesn't end in fulfillment. It ends in emptiness.

Think about it. How many times have you bought something that you thought would make you happy, only for the joy to dissipate a few days later? The new shoes lose their shine. The new phone gets replaced with the next model. The vacation snaps are buried under work emails.

You were promised happiness, but what you got was a temporary high, followed by the inevitable crash.

And yet, we keep chasing it.

The marketing industry has perfected this cycle. It has turned us into addicts. It has created a world where consumerism is the religion, and the gods are the brands, the products, the advertisements. We don't just buy things anymore—we buy identities. We buy social status. We buy validation. This isn't about wanting things. It's about wanting to feel like we matter.

Why do we keep buying things we don't need? Why do we obsess over stuff that doesn't bring us real happiness?

It's simple. We're conditioned to. It's in the air we breathe, the media we consume, the world we live in. Consumerism has become the very fabric of our existence, and it tells us that we are not enough without it.

You're not just a person; you're a brand. You're a consumer, a product of society, and everything you buy is a way to reflect how much you matter in a world that values things more than people. But the worst part? It's all an illusion. You are not what you buy. You are not your possessions. You are not the size of your house, the car you drive, or the clothes you wear.

But here's the catch. The system works because we believe it. We buy into the idea that more is better. And once we start buying, it's impossible to stop. This isn't about you. This is about the system. The system that makes money from your emptiness. The system that keeps you coming back for more, and every time you walk out of that store, or click that "buy now" button, you're feeding the machine. It doesn't matter if you're in debt. It doesn't matter if you're overwhelmed. It doesn't matter if you can't sleep at night because you're worried about the next bill. Because the machine needs you to buy more. It thrives on your addiction. The more you buy, the more they profit. The more they profit, the more they control.

The problem with this addiction is that we've been trained to need it. Consumer culture has programmed us to believe that happiness is a transaction. That love, satisfaction, and success are things you purchase. You're taught that if you buy the right things, you'll finally feel worthy, important, powerful. But this is where the addiction becomes dangerous. The more you consume, the more you are consumed by the need to consume. You lose sight of yourself. You forget what makes you truly happy. You get caught in a cycle of spending to feel good. You buy the things you think you want, and before you know it, you've sold yourself out. You've given up your peace, your time, and your identity for a fleeting fix that fades the moment you realize you're still not enough.

It's not just about stuff. It's about validation. In a world where consumerism is king, we've been taught that what we own defines us. You're not seen for who you are. You're seen for what you can afford. Your success is determined by the number of things you own, the brands you wear, the car you drive, the vacations you post about. These are the markers of success. And if you don't have them, you're nothing. You're irrelevant.

This is the lie that fuels the addiction.

You're not addicted to money. You're addicted to the feeling that money can prove your worth.

But this isn't your fault.

This is a systemic addiction. One that's been carefully crafted and meticulously marketed. It's not just the ads, the magazines, or the influencers. It's the way consumerism has infiltrated every part of our lives. It's in the way we've been programmed to associate stuff with happiness, wealth with value, and brands with identity. It's how we've been taught to chase the next purchase, the next big thing, because that's what we've been told will make us feel good.

But it won't. It never does.

You will never feel fulfilled by purchasing things. You will never feel complete because of a new pair of shoes or the latest tech gadget. These things are not the solution. They're distractions. They are the tools used by consumer culture to keep you distracted, to keep you empty, to keep you coming back for more.

But the truth is, you don't need more. You need freedom. You need peace. You need contentment.

And you'll never find it in a shopping mall or online store.

The more you buy, the more you give up who you really are.

"You're not buying things – you're buying temporary permission to feel worthy."

THE FINANCIALIZED SELF

In today's world, your value is no longer about who you are. It's about what you have. It's about the number in your bank account, the car you drive, the neighborhood you live in, the brand of clothes you wear, and the status you project. We live in a society where your self-worth is increasingly defined by your financial success—and we've been conditioned to believe that money is everything.

From the moment we are born, we are told that money is the key to freedom, security, and happiness. We are taught to chase it, to worship it, to define ourselves by it. The message is clear: if you don't have money, you don't have value. And if you don't have value, you don't matter. This is the system we live in. This is the trap we've all been born into.

But what happens when we start to believe it? What happens when we start to tie our identity to money, to wealth, to the things we own? What happens when we start to see ourselves as nothing more than the sum of our possessions? We lose ourselves. We lose our sense of who we really are and replace it with a false, financialized self.

The concept of financialized self-worth didn't just happen overnight. It was carefully built into the very fabric of society. It's a product of centuries of conditioning—first by wealthy elites who wanted to ensure that their power remained unchallenged, and later by media, advertising, and consumer culture that taught us that more money equals more happiness. This belief has become so deeply embedded that most of us never even question it.

The idea that money equals worth is so normalized that we hardly even notice it. We are measured by our income, our possessions, and our financial success. When we meet someone, one of the first things we ask is, "What do you do?" Not to learn about their passions, their dreams, their soul—but to assess their value. What they do determines how important they are. How much money they make determines how much respect they are entitled to.

This is the dangerous intersection between wealth and identity. Money is no longer just a means of exchange. It's a scorecard, a way of measuring a person's value and importance. This is the financialized self. And the worst part? It doesn't just affect those who have too much money—it affects everyone. Because once money is tied to your identity, you never feel like you have enough. You always feel less than. No matter how much you make, you are always chasing the next milestone—the next promotion, the next purchase, the next level of wealth. Because the system tells you that until you reach that next level, you are not worthy.

But here's the truth: your worth has nothing to do with money. It has nothing to do with your paycheck, your job title, your assets, or your bank balance. It has everything to do with who you are as a person—the depth of your character, the kindness you show, the way you treat others, the joy you bring to the world. That is your true worth. But we have forgotten that. We have traded it for the false promise of more.

As long as we live in a world where financial success is the primary measure of a person's value, we will continue to fall into the trap of comparison. We constantly compare ourselves to others—how much they have, how much we don't. This is why the rich get richer and the poor get poorer: not just because of systemic issues, but because we have been conditioned to value others based on their financial success, and by extension, value ourselves based on how we measure up to them.

How many times have you felt inadequate because someone else has more? How many times have you measured your success against someone else's wealth, their career achievements, their lifestyle? Every time you see someone with something you don't have—whether it's the perfect house, the latest gadget, the luxury vacation—you're reminded that you don't measure up. And this isn't just about envy or jealousy. It's about the fact that society has taught you that you are worth less if you don't have those things.

This is the cycle of the financialized self. We chase more, not because we need it, but because we have been taught to believe that having more makes us better. But as long as we keep comparing ourselves to others, we will never feel like we are enough. No matter how much we have, it will always be less than someone else. And so we keep chasing. We keep accumulating. We keep selling our souls in an attempt to meet someone else's idea of success.

But the reality is that money does not define you. You are not your paycheck, your possessions, or your status. You are not the things you buy or the brands you wear. You are you—a human being with dreams, passions, and experiences that have nothing to do with how much you make. The more you tie your identity to money, the more you lose touch with who you truly are.

The damage done by the financialized self is not just emotional. It is psychological. It is a deep psychological wound that distorts our sense of self. The more we define ourselves by what we have, the more empty we become. It is a constant chase, and the chase is never satisfying. Every time we achieve something—whether it's a pay raise, a promotion, or the purchase of something new—we experience a brief high. But that high never lasts. The satisfaction fades, and we are left with the same hunger, the same emptiness, the same lack of fulfillment.

This is the addiction of consumerism. This is the addiction of the financialized self. The chase never ends. No matter how much we have, it is never enough. And that feeling of lack becomes internalized. It becomes a deep belief that we are never enough, just as we are. We start to believe that who we are is measured by what we have, and we forget that the true measure of who we are lies in our values, our actions, and our relationships—not in the size of our paycheck.

We are not our financial statements. We are not our job titles or the size of our house. But the more we let these things define us, the more we lose our sense of true self-worth. We are taught that more is better—that more stuff, more money, and more status will make us feel complete. But the truth is, more doesn't fill the void. The void is inside you. And until you stop measuring yourself by what you own, and start measuring yourself by who you are, you will always feel empty.

But how do you begin to break free from this cycle? How do you stop defining yourself by your financial success?

The first step is awareness. You have to recognize that you have been conditioned to believe that money equals worth. You have to realize that you are enough—right now, as you are. You don't need more money, more stuff, or more accolades to be worthy. The second step is detachment. Start detaching your identity from what you own. Let go of the need to keep up with others. Let go of the need for external validation. Start focusing on what truly matters—your relationships, your passions, your personal growth. The third step is contentment. Begin practicing contentment with what you have, without the desire for more. Recognize that enough is enough—and that true happiness does not come from accumulation. It comes from peace. It comes from within.

"You weren't born addicted - you were groomed by a system that profits from your emptiness."

REFLECTION QUESTIONS

- When did you first feel that your value was linked to your income?
- How much of your life has been spent chasing more money rather than seeking inner peace or purpose?
- What would you do differently if your worth wasn't attached to your paycheck?
- How can you begin to change the way you view success?
- What's the first step in unhooking yourself from this addiction?

CHAPTER THREE

THE EMOTIONAL HIJACK

"Your emotions aren't yours. They've been outsourced to a system that profits from your panic."

MONEY'S EMOTIONAL BLUEPRINT

You don't remember the first time money controlled your emotions. But your body does. Your nervous system remembers the tone in your parents' voices when the bills came. It remembers the tension that wrapped around dinner conversations like a snake. It remembers the sudden silence when someone asked, "Can we afford it?" and no one answered. Long before you understood what money was, you learned how it made people feel. And how it was allowed to make you feel.

No one had to teach you that money equals stress. You absorbed it by watching your parents look at each other with fear in their eyes when rent was due. You felt it when they snapped at you for asking for a toy. You learned early that money made people angry, worried, quiet, or cold. Money wasn't just currency—it was emotion. You didn't grow up with financial literacy. You grew up with financial tension. And that's far more dangerous.

Money became emotional before it ever became logical. It didn't matter whether your family had a little or a lot. It mattered how money was spoken about, how it was treated, how it was weaponized in silence. Maybe you were told not to ask for things because "money doesn't grow on trees." Maybe your needs were dismissed because "we're not made of cash." Or maybe no one talked about money at all—leaving you to guess, to fill in the blanks, to assume that discomfort was normal. That was your training. That was the start of your emotional hijack.

We don't talk enough about how children internalize financial trauma. Not the kind that shows up on credit reports. The kind that shows up in how you flinch when talking about debt. In how your throat tightens when someone says "let's split the bill." In how you feel physically sick when checking your bank balance. These aren't just habits. These are scars. They came from years of learning that your worth was tied to whether your parents could afford to say yes to you. That love came with conditions. That survival came with silence. That abundance was for someone else.

This is the emotional blueprint of money, and it gets written in childhood—etched into your psychology, woven into your sense of self, often without a single direct conversation. Instead of learning how to relate to money, we learned how to react to it. We were trained to fear it, to crave it, to feel ashamed of wanting it, and to judge others by how much of it they had. And we carried that training into adulthood like an invisible bag of bricks.

If you grew up poor, money became a symbol of humiliation. You knew what it felt like to be told "no" in front of your friends. You learned how to make up excuses about why you couldn't go on the class trip, why you didn't bring lunch money, why you wore the same shoes every year. You learned how to shrink. How to disappear. How to pretend you didn't care. But deep down, you did. Because being broke wasn't just a circumstance—it became your identity. And that shame didn't go away when you started earning. It just dressed itself differently.

If you grew up in a household that had money but never talked about it, the message was just as damaging. You were told, without words, that discussing money was impolite. That needing it was weak. That not having it was a personal failure. You learned how to perform wealth, but not how to understand it. And that performance became your cage. It became the mask you wore even when you were drowning in debt, even when your world was crumbling, because admitting you didn't have control meant admitting you were less than.

Then came school, where the social hierarchy was built not on character, but consumption. The kids who had the new clothes, the expensive backpacks, the latest tech—those were the ones who seemed to matter. You noticed. Everyone did. No teacher had to say it out loud. You saw who was picked first. You saw who got invited to the parties. And you learned that money didn't just buy things. It bought visibility. It bought power. It bought belonging.

It's in childhood that you start equating financial status with social worth. That association is never accidental. It's cultural. It's systemic. And it's relentless. You are told in subtle, unspoken ways that being rich makes you admirable, and being poor makes you invisible. So, you start measuring yourself. You compare. You compete. You feel like you're falling behind before you even start. And no one tells you it's all an illusion.

What's worse is how early we begin confusing financial stability with emotional safety. When you grow up watching adults panic over bills, you internalize the idea that chaos is normal unless there's money. So, you chase money not just for comfort, but for emotional survival. You start believing that if you just have enough, the panic will stop. That if you just earn more, you'll finally be able to breathe. But the truth is brutal: most people never feel safe, no matter how much they make. Because the emotional blueprint is still running the show.

By the time you earn your first paycheck, the hijack is complete. You feel a rush, not just from the money—but from what it symbolizes. You made it. You matter now. You're not dependent anymore. You're becoming the thing you were told would save you: financially independent. But even then, there's anxiety. You hold onto it. You check your account obsessively. You track every expense. Or maybe you spend recklessly, trying to drown out the years of deprivation. Either way, you're not free. You're reacting. You're reliving your past with every dollar that enters or leaves your life.

And if you fail? If you lose a job, miss a rent payment, go into debt? The emotions come back stronger than ever. Shame. Fear. Panic. Because you weren't just taught that money is important—you were taught that **money is moral**. That not having it means you've done something wrong. That you're lazy. Undisciplined. Broken. This is the legacy of a society that measures character through credit scores and ambition through bank statements.

So you hustle. You perform. You build the image. You chase the next raise, the next client, the next side hustle. But deep down, you're still that kid—afraid to ask for something, afraid to need, afraid to be told no again. You've grown up, but the blueprint hasn't. And until you rewrite it, money will always own your emotions. It will dictate your joy. It will define your relationships. It will decide how you see yourself.

Rewriting the blueprint doesn't mean rejecting money. It means confronting how money shaped you. It means asking uncomfortable questions: Who taught me how to feel about money? Whose shame am I still carrying? What parts of my identity are built on fear, not truth? It means going back, not to re-live the past, but to untangle the lies.

Because here's the truth: money is not a measure of your value. It's not a reflection of your intelligence, your work ethic, or your potential. It's a system. And that system has infected your emotional world. It made you believe that your worth can be bought. That your safety depends on numbers. That your dignity has a price tag.

But you are not a price. You are not a paycheck. You are not a product.

You are still in there—beneath the programming, beneath the panic, beneath the debt. The version of you that existed before you learned to shrink, before you learned to perform, before money became your master. That version didn't care about brands or bank accounts. That version just wanted to be safe. To be loved. To be enough.

And the good news? That version never left. It's just been buried under years of emotional manipulation. Reclaiming it starts with seeing the blueprint for what it is: someone else's map of your worth.

You can burn it. You can start over. But not by earning more.

By remembering who you were before they taught you to measure yourself in numbers.

SHAME AND FEAR

Shame is a quiet killer. It doesn't show up screaming in your face. It creeps in with every declined transaction, every late bill, every paycheck that doesn't stretch far enough. It sits beside you while you scroll through people's filtered lifestyles and whispers, "You're behind." It follows you into the grocery store when you silently take items out of your cart before reaching the checkout. It's in the way you avoid eye contact with the waiter when you can't tip what you know they deserve. Shame doesn't come from money. It comes from the emotional value we've been taught to attach to it.

Fear isn't loud either. It's the shallow breath you take when your landlord texts you. It's the silent panic when you log into your banking app and wait for the number to load. It's the lump in your throat when a friend suggests splitting the bill and you smile, even though you know you can't afford it. This is the unspoken emotional tax we pay for living in a system that equates dignity with income and visibility with wealth. You don't just fear being broke. You fear being seen as broke.

No one talks about this. Not really. Because shame and fear make you quiet. They make you withdraw. They make you pretend. They convince you that this is just how it is. That everyone else has figured it out and you're the only one struggling. But that's the lie. That's the trap. The truth is, most people are one paycheck away from panic, one unexpected bill away from spiraling, one job loss away from crisis. But we've been trained to perform—to smile through it, to post the highlight reel, to keep hustling like we're okay.

Money doesn't just buy comfort. It buys the permission to be at peace. When you don't have it, you don't just feel poor—you feel powerless. And that powerlessness is soaked in shame. You start believing that if you were smarter, more disciplined, more responsible, you'd be doing better. That if you worked harder, managed better, saved more, you wouldn't be stuck. And instead of pointing to a system that's rigged, you point the blame inward. That's what shame does. It convinces you the problem is you.

Where does that belief come from? It's fed to you from the beginning. Every time someone says "money doesn't grow on trees," every time a kid is told they need to "make something of themselves," every time someone says "they must've done something wrong to be in debt"—those words plant the seed. And that seed grows into internalized worthlessness. You start to believe that struggling is a moral failure. That wealth equals virtue and poverty equals weakness. But those ideas are engineered. They are designed to keep you running.

Fear keeps the machine running. Fear of eviction. Fear of medical bills. Fear of saying no. Fear of not measuring up. And shame makes sure you don't talk about it. That's how systems stay intact—not with bars, but with beliefs. Beliefs so deeply embedded that you carry them like gospel.

Shame is why you buy things you can't afford—to hide how little you feel inside. It's why you dress up debt as ambition. It's why you spend money to belong. You're not buying things. You're buying permission to feel enough. You're trying to outrun the internal story that says, "If people knew the truth, they'd think less of me." So you perform. You build the illusion. You keep up.

But the cost is enormous. The emotional weight of financial fear is heavy, and most of us are carrying it silently. The anxiety, the insomnia, the irritability, the exhaustion—it's not laziness. It's not weakness. It's emotional fatigue from constantly living in financial survival mode. From being on guard all the time. From knowing that one wrong move could ruin everything. This isn't just about money. It's about your nervous system being hijacked by capitalism.

Even success doesn't erase the fear. You finally get the promotion, the raise, the "good job." But instead of feeling safe, you feel terrified of losing it. The system trains you not to rest. It trains you to see rest as laziness, contentment as complacency, and stillness as falling behind. And so the shame never truly leaves—it just evolves. From "I don't have enough" to "I might lose what I've earned." And the fear grows louder. Because now, there's something to protect. Now, the stakes feel higher. Now, the panic has more room to stretch.

We're not just talking about being broke. We're talking about being emotionally bankrupt. About what it does to your sense of identity when your survival is always hanging by a thread. About what it does to your relationships when you're afraid to tell the truth. About what it does to your self-respect when you have to choose between dignity and making rent. These are the choices people make every day. Quietly. Desperately. Alone.

But the shame doesn't come from the reality. It comes from the illusion that this is your fault. That if you were better, you wouldn't be here. But who benefits from that belief? Not you. Who gains when you blame yourself instead of the systems that set you up to fail? Not you. Who profits when you stay quiet, overwork, and keep pretending everything is okay? They do. The people selling you solutions to problems they created. The corporations that market "financial wellness" while underpaying their staff. The industries built on your fear.

This is the emotional violence of capitalism. And the worst part is how invisible it is. We don't see the system—we see our own reflection. And we internalize its cruelty as our identity. That's what shame does. It makes oppression feel personal. It makes structural inequality look like individual failure. And that is its most powerful trick.

So you hide. You hide the bills. You hide the struggle. You don't talk about the overdraft notices or the bounced checks or the credit cards maxed out from survival. You smile. You grind. You post curated content. But inside, you're breaking. Because you were never meant to carry this weight. And yet, here you are, convincing yourself that carrying it makes you strong.

But real strength isn't pretending you're not drowning. It's admitting the water is deep. It's saying, "This isn't just about me." It's unlearning the shame that was handed to you by a system designed to profit from your silence. That's where freedom begins —not with more money, but with less self-blame.

Fear is not weakness. It's a response to instability. It's your body trying to keep you safe. But when your entire life becomes about managing fear, you lose the ability to dream, to rest, to be human. That's what they don't tell you. That shame and fear are not flaws. They're symptoms. And when a whole society is sick with them, it means the culture is broken. Not the people.

This section isn't about fixing your budget. It's about giving you your humanity back. You are not weak for feeling overwhelmed. You are not a failure because you're behind. You are not broken because you're scared. You are reacting to a world that teaches you to attach your soul to your salary. That's not failure. That's survival. And now that you can see it for what it is, you have a choice.

You can keep running. Or you can stop. You can keep performing. Or you can start telling the truth. You can keep chasing security through a system that feeds on your panic—or you can reclaim your peace by refusing to play.

You are not alone in this. Everyone around you is carrying their version of this fear. They just don't say it out loud. But once someone breaks the silence, the shame starts to die. And the system loses its grip.

The truth is ugly. But it's also liberating. You've been punished for not having enough, and punished for wanting more. But the real crime is that you were taught to feel worthless because of it. That ends now.

"You didn't learn finance – you inherited fear wrapped in silence."

PRIDE AND EGO

If shame and fear are the whips that keep you running, pride is the sugar that keeps you hooked. It's seductive. It doesn't hurt— at least not at first. It feels good. It feels earned. You hit the target, you close the deal, you walk into a room knowing your outfit cost more than their rent. You don't feel shame in that moment. You feel power. You feel seen.

But that's the illusion. Because what you're really feeling isn't self-worth. It's **ego**—propped up, puffed up, swollen with validation that came wrapped in currency. You think you're standing tall on solid ground. But you're standing on receipts. And receipts burn fast.

It starts innocently. You work hard. You earn something. The world claps. You feel proud—and you should. There's nothing wrong with pride in honest effort. But somewhere along the way, that pride mutates. It stops being about what you did and starts being about what you have. It becomes less about who you are and more about how others perceive you.

That's when ego slips in. Quietly. Elegantly. Like a virus in expensive cologne. It tells you that success makes you better. That wealth makes you wise. That having more means you've figured out something other people haven't. And if you're not careful, you believe it.

This is the great lie of capitalism: that your material status is a reflection of your inner worth. That the wealthy are more disciplined, more focused, more evolved. That poverty is the result of laziness or lack of intelligence. This lie fuels meritocracy. It fuels toxic pride. It's the gasoline for hustle culture. But it's a fabrication. A social fantasy. A fragile, toxic framework designed to protect those at the top from guilt, and those at the bottom from asking the right questions.

Wealth doesn't make you worthy. It makes you lucky. Or it makes you connected. Or it makes you complicit in a system that rewards exploitation. And sure, sometimes it makes you strategic, relentless, bold. But worth? Worth isn't bought. It isn't stacked in portfolios or flashed in status symbols. Worth is intrinsic. And if your worth depends on how much you earn or own, then you never owned yourself to begin with.

But let's be honest—ego is addictive. Because when the money flows, so does the attention. You're praised. Admired. Invited. Suddenly your words carry more weight. Your presence shifts the room. People listen differently. And you start to believe it. That you're smarter. That your time is more valuable. That your opinion is more informed. And without realizing it, you become a mirror of the very system that once crushed you.

That's how trauma works. You go from victim to participant. From underdog to overseer. You recreate the power dynamic that hurt you, but this time, you're on the winning side. And it feels like justice. But it's not. It's just inversion. You've changed costumes, not systems.

The ego will always choose pride over truth. It will always cling to the illusion of superiority, because deep down, it remembers the fear. It remembers being broke. Being ignored. Being insecure. And it never wants to feel that again. So it builds armor. It calls that armor confidence. But it's not confidence. It's fear dressed in Gucci.

True confidence doesn't need an audience. It doesn't need net worth statements or validation from strangers. It's quiet. It's rooted. It can walk into any room without the need to prove a thing. But ego? Ego needs applause. Ego needs to be seen. Ego needs to **win**—even if no one else is playing.

And when pride becomes your identity, everything becomes a competition. You start comparing yourself to everyone. You judge people for what they drive, where they eat, what they wear. You surround yourself with those who reinforce your status, and you push away anyone who challenges it. You build a life on hierarchy. And you become afraid—not of failure, but of falling.

Because once your value is tied to your financial position, every downturn becomes an identity crisis. Every market crash feels personal. Every demotion feels like humiliation. The ego can't handle uncertainty. So you work harder. You build bigger. You protect the castle. But the moat isn't filled with water—it's filled with loneliness, anxiety, and the gnawing truth that none of it is real.

Look closely at the people who worship their wealth. They don't sleep well. They don't laugh freely. Their conversations are resumes. Their friendships are transactions. Their relationships are often power plays dressed as love. They don't trust easily. And they don't rest—because resting feels like death when your value is performance.

This is the cost of the illusion. Pride may elevate you in public, but it isolates you in private. It demands perfection. It leaves no room for vulnerability. And eventually, the pressure becomes unbearable. Because no amount of external success can silence the internal question: "If I lost all this, would I still be worthy?"

Ego doesn't like that question. It panics. It lashes out. It buys more. It works more. It posts more. But your soul knows. Your soul remembers who you were before the chase began. And it aches for that version of you. The one who didn't measure life in numbers. The one who didn't mistake status for safety.

You're not broken for craving pride. We all want to feel seen. We all want to feel valued. But the system taught you to seek it through ownership, not through essence. Through projection, not through presence. And now you're here—burned out, over-worked, addicted to productivity, terrified of stillness.

Let me say this clearly: **There is nothing wrong with success. But there is something deeply wrong with needing success to feel like someone.**

When your identity is fused with your income, you become vulnerable to every financial storm. You become volatile. You mistake visibility for love. You lose yourself in the character you built to survive. And slowly, the real you disappears under layers of armor.

But the truth is still there. It's just buried under the noise.

You are not more valuable because you make more. You are not wiser because you earn more. You are not superior because you can afford more.

You're just playing a different role in the same performance.

You can opt out of that role. You can strip away the gold-plated identity and ask the harder questions. Who am I without the applause? Who am I without the performance? What part of me is real, and what part is just marketing?

These questions are terrifying. They threaten the ego. They unravel the pride. But they lead to freedom. Because once you untangle who you are from what you earn, you can finally breathe without needing to prove anything.

You can stop judging others for how much they have. You can stop judging yourself for how much you don't. You can show up to your life—not as a brand, but as a person.

The illusion is strong. It's reinforced everywhere. In magazines, in boardrooms, on stages, in families. But it's still a lie. And like all lies, it crumbles under honest scrutiny.

So be honest.

You were taught that wealth makes you better. But does it? Or does it just make you louder?

You were taught that pride comes from achievement. But does it? Or is it just armor against the fear of being seen as less?

You were taught to chase status. But for what? To impress people who are also pretending?

This is your chance to stop pretending. To stop performing. To let go of the illusion and meet yourself again—not as an earner, a hustler, a brand, or a provider—but as a human being who deserves love, respect, and rest. Without needing to win anything first.

ENVY, GUILT, AND EMOTIONAL BANKRUPTCY

You envy them. You know you do. The ones who seem to have it all—the house, the brand deals, the lifestyle, the perfect holiday photos. You scroll, and something inside you knots. A mixture of admiration, resentment, longing, and shame. You tell yourself you're happy for them. You might even hit the like button. But deep down, it stings. It hits that raw, sensitive part of you that still believes you're behind.

And this isn't just jealousy. This is systemic. This is programmed. This is **capitalist envy**, built to keep you feeling not just inadequate, but hungry. Hungry for more. Hungry for their life. Hungry for the version of you that looks like them. That's what envy does under capitalism—it tells you that if you had what they had, you would finally feel whole. Safe. Visible.

But envy isn't about the objects. Not really. It's not the car or the vacation or the followers. It's about the emotions you've attached to those things. You believe their money gives them permission to rest. To be loved. To be admired. You're not envious of what they have—you're envious of what you imagine they feel. That's the lie.

Because no one posts the panic. No one uploads the sleepless nights. No one shares the debt, the performance fatigue, the quiet dread that it could all collapse. Social envy is built on edited footage. You're comparing your behind-the-scenes to someone else's highlight reel, and the system relies on that comparison to sell you things. To keep you striving. To keep you ashamed of still wanting more.

You've been taught to see envy as a flaw. Something petty. Immature. But envy under capitalism is weaponized dissatisfaction. It's not about hate. It's about longing. It's about being constantly shown a life you were told you could have if you just work harder—but that somehow always seems out of reach.

You don't envy wealth. You envy peace. You envy the feeling of enough. The idea that someone out there gets to stop running. And you carry that feeling like a sickness. Quietly. Daily.

Then there's guilt.

The guilt of wanting more when you already have so much. The guilt of not being further ahead. The guilt of spending money on yourself. The guilt of not having enough to help your family. The guilt of being able to help, but choosing not to. The guilt of succeeding while others are drowning. The guilt of resting when others are grinding.

This guilt isn't virtue. It's conditioning. You were trained to carry it. Trained to feel bad for wanting better, and worse for getting it. Especially if you come from struggle. Especially if you made it out of a cycle others are still trapped in. You feel responsible. Accountable. Like your success came at the cost of someone else's suffering. Because in some ways, it did.

That's the weight of generational pain. Of upward mobility. Of the "I made it" story that comes with a silent footnote: but I left people behind.

So you overgive. You overwork. You minimize your needs. You stay silent about your wins. You sabotage yourself because the guilt of thriving feels heavier than the pain of staying small.

And when you fail, you feel it too. The guilt of not being enough. Not providing enough. Not being the version of yourself you told everyone you'd become. You measure your love by your bank account. Your usefulness by your income. Your relationships by your ability to pay. And when you can't? You crumble inside. You withdraw. You start to believe that your very presence is a burden.

That's emotional bankruptcy.

Not the kind that hits your credit score—the kind that eats your sense of worth.

You wake up tired. You move through your day numb. You smile when you're supposed to. You hit the deadlines. You show up. But your joy is gone. Your creativity is dry. Your sense of self is foggy. You're not living—you're functioning. You're meeting expectations. Paying dues. Managing image. Chasing numbers. And somewhere deep inside, a voice whispers, "This isn't what life is supposed to feel like."

You want to rest, but rest feels unsafe. You want to slow down, but slow feels like failing. You want to speak honestly, but the shame would choke you. So you keep going. And you call it strength. But it's not strength. It's survival. It's burnout wearing a blazer.

Emotional bankruptcy is what happens when your internal life has been mortgaged to maintain the appearance of success. When your joy is always pending. When love, rest, peace, identity —all of it feels like something you have to earn. As if you don't deserve those things just by being alive.

You start believing that your emotional world must align with your financial world. That if you're broke, you're not allowed to be happy. That if you're in debt, you don't deserve joy. That if you haven't "made it," you don't get to feel proud. You've internalized capitalism's rules for emotion. And those rules are killing you.

You were born worthy. But you were trained to believe that worth comes with proof—paystubs, promotions, property, passive income. You're so used to measuring yourself in digits that you forgot how to feel proud of yourself without an invoice to back it up.

So what do you do?

You fake it. You put on the mask. You say the right things. You play the game. Because everyone else is doing it. And no one wants to be the first to say, "I'm drowning." No one wants to admit that the chase never ends. That the joy never really lands. That the feeling of enough is always delayed, postponed, rescheduled for a tomorrow that never comes.

You envy people who look like they've figured it out. You feel guilty for not being one of them. And inside, you're emotionally bankrupt—because you've spent years investing in an identity that doesn't belong to you. An identity built on hustle. On appearance. On status. An identity that can't survive in stillness, can't breathe without applause, can't rest without permission.

You've been taught to monetize your emotions. To turn pain into profit. To turn healing into content. To turn rest into productivity. Even your mental health is now branded and sold back to you as a "journey." But you're not a product. You're not a profile. You're not a brand.

You're a human being who was told from the beginning that your worth was conditional.

That's the real crime. That's the rot in the foundation. You've been fed a diet of shame and fear, guilt and envy, and called it personal growth. But growth without healing is just performance. And performance is not life. It's a prison with spotlight lighting.

You don't have to envy anymore. You don't have to carry the guilt. You don't have to trade your emotions for a seat at the table. Because real worth doesn't need translation. It doesn't need proof. It just is.

Let that be enough. Even if it's messy. Even if it's quiet. Even if no one claps. Especially then.

"If your joy needs a paycheck to exist, it was never joy—it was approval in disguise."

REFLECTION QUESTIONS

- When did money first make you feel ashamed?
- What fear is driving your pursuit of more?
- Who are you trying to prove your worth to—and why?
- What does success look like without a number attached?
- Are your emotional highs and lows coming from life—or from your wallet?

CHAPTER FOUR

SECURITY OR ADDICTION?

"What you call security is just addiction with better branding."

THE FALSE PROMISE OF SAFETY

You were told security was the goal. That once you earned enough, saved enough, planned enough—you'd finally be able to exhale. They dangled that dream in front of you like a prize. Work hard. Be smart. Follow the rules. And in the end, you'll be safe.

You believed them.

And that belief cost you more than money. It cost you trust. It cost you time. It cost you peace.

Because here's the truth they never said out loud: safety is the drug, not the destination. They sell you the feeling of it, not the substance. You are meant to chase it forever, never arriving. Because the moment you feel truly safe, you stop needing them. And the system can't survive that.

So they move the line.

Ten years ago, they said a full-time job would do it. Now you need a side hustle. Then they said owning a home meant stability. Now your mortgage is a trap. Then they told you a degree meant security. Now you're swimming in debt with nothing but a framed receipt on your wall.

Every generation is given a new flavor of the same lie: "This path will make you safe." But the finish line keeps vanishing. That's not by accident. That's by design.

The economy doesn't run on certainty. It runs on anxiety. And you? You're the battery. Not because you're lazy or weak or broken. But because you were told that security is something to earn, to sacrifice for, to crawl toward.

And the moment you get close? They raise the price.

They told you a savings account would give you peace. But then inflation robbed you silently. They told you retirement would be the reward—but moved the goalposts till it became a moving grave. They told you a steady job was protection—until your boss outsourced your position and called it "strategy." Every form of promised safety was built to feel just stable enough to keep you from questioning. But never stable enough to truly rest.

So you keep chasing. Not money. Not luxury. Permission to stop fearing.

But fear is the currency here. It's what keeps you from taking risks. From leaving jobs that poison you. From walking away from lives you no longer recognize. Fear makes you predictable. Fear makes you manageable. Fear makes you behave.

And they sell security like a cure. They offer it in products, insurance policies, emergency funds, gated communities, bulletproof careers. But those things don't make you safe. They just make you dependent.

You want to know why you never feel secure? Because you were never meant to. The economy doesn't benefit from your stability. It benefits from your doubt. The more you worry, the more you spend. The more you fear, the more you obey. The more uncertain you feel, the more control they have. Real safety would be catastrophic to this system.

So instead, they teach you to hoard. To prepare. To shrink. To chase safety like it's something outside yourself—when the truth is, the only real safety you'll ever know is the kind you build inside your own mind. But no one teaches that. Because it can't be taxed. It can't be monetized. It can't be sold back to you as a product.

They teach you to insure everything but your soul.

How many decisions have you made out of fear, dressed up as logic?

How many times have you stayed in places that drained you because you told yourself it was "secure"? How many relationships have you endured because the finances made it easier than leaving? How many talents have you buried because they didn't guarantee a paycheck? How many dreams have you downgraded into tasks, into roles, into routines that look responsible but feel like slow death?

They said responsibility would bring security. But all it brought was exhaustion.

You learned to trade your imagination for predictability. You learned to tolerate monotony in exchange for stability. You learned to measure your life by how protected it was from worst-case scenarios. But what kind of life is that? What kind of freedom is that?

They told you safety was noble. But it was never about nobility. It was about obedience. It was about keeping you inside a cage you were too tired to question. A cage lined with titles, benefits, plans, and promotions that looked like progress but felt like sedation.

And if you did start to question it? If you ever tried to take a leap?

You were punished. Not always directly. But emotionally. Socially. You were called reckless. Irresponsible. Immature. People asked, "Are you sure that's smart?" "What if it doesn't work out?" "But what about your pension?" They weren't worried for you. They were afraid for themselves. Because if you proved that safety was a lie, they'd have to face it too.

So they mocked the artists. They dismissed the wanderers. They judged the dropouts, the freelancers, the ones who said, "No thanks. I'll find another way."

Because anyone who refused the security myth was a threat to the illusion. And the illusion is sacred.

But here's the part no one tells you:

Even the safest path breaks. Even the most responsible plan crumbles. Even the most secure job can ghost you without warning. And when it does, all that sacrifice means nothing. You're just another number. Another "unforeseen layoff." Another body that got left behind when the market shifted.

And still, they'll tell you to trust the system. Still, they'll tell you to "stick to the plan."

But whose plan is it?

Yours? Or the one they gave you to keep you too scared to build your own?

Security wasn't meant to free you. It was meant to **numb you**.

You've been taught to confuse peace with paralysis. Stillness with safety. Conformity with wisdom. But real peace doesn't come from a padded cage.

It comes from knowing you could lose everything and still be yourself.

That's the kind of safety they can't sell you.

So what now?

You start by telling the truth.

You admit that the chase never ends. You admit that the plan doesn't work. You admit that you've been living under a spell called "someday." Someday I'll have enough. Someday I'll feel calm. Someday I'll be ready.

But someday is a script. A stall tactic. A form of compliance written in calendar invites and broken promises.

You reclaim that script.

You stop making decisions based on what keeps you from falling. You start choosing what brings you to life. You stop asking what's smart and start asking what's true. You let go of the obsession with fallback plans. You stop trying to secure the whole future. You start learning how to feel safe in the moment, not in the spreadsheet.

And yes—it's terrifying. Because when you stop pretending the system works, you're left with space. Uncertainty. Void. But that void is holy. That space is real. That's where your life actually begins.

You weren't born to chase safety. You were born to build something no one can take from you. Not a job. Not a title. Not a plan. But a way of living that doesn't require constant escape.

You don't have to be fearless to begin.

You just have to stop letting fear be the reason you stay.

FEAR AS DESIGN

You've been told that the fear you feel around money is just part of being an adult. That it's normal to worry about rent. That stress over bills means you're responsible. That waking up anxious about tomorrow is simply a byproduct of maturity. But that's not true. That's propaganda. What you're experiencing is not emotional immaturity or personal mismanagement. It's conditioning. And that conditioning is not a bug in the system. It's the blueprint.

This economy doesn't function despite your fear. It functions because of it.

Fear isn't a side effect. It's the fuel.

They call it uncertainty, volatility, market instability. But what they never call it is intentional. They want you to believe that recessions are natural disasters, that inflation is an unavoidable phenomenon, that layoffs are unfortunate outcomes. But that's a lie told so often we've stopped questioning it. These are not economic "storms." They are scheduled evacuations of your security.

It begins at the structural level. You're born into a framework where the cost of basic existence—food, shelter, education, healthcare—is just high enough to keep you reaching, but never high enough to justify rebellion. You are introduced to scarcity from the first time your parents say "we can't afford that." And before you can even pronounce capitalism, you're already a dependent of its psychology.

The system introduces fear early and normalizes it constantly. You learn to fear falling behind in school, because it determines the kind of job you'll get. You learn to fear bad credit scores, because it dictates your access to everything from housing to emergency funds. You learn to fear gaps in your résumé, as if time to breathe is a crime. Every pause is framed as a failure. Every question is discouraged unless it reinforces the hustle.

You're taught to fear the consequences of financial collapse more than the symptoms of spiritual decay. They never asked if you felt alive in your job. They only asked if it came with a dental plan.

That's how deep the manipulation runs. The economy doesn't just threaten you—it convinces you that your reaction to its threats is evidence of your maturity.

When you're anxious, you're considered responsible. When you're overworked, you're called committed. When you're burned out, they reward you with praise for "pushing through." At no point are you asked whether any of this is human.

And that's the point.

This economy is not human-centered. It is fear-centered. Every institution is designed to keep you slightly uncomfortable, slightly confused, slightly behind. Just enough that you keep grinding, but never enough that you truly revolt.

Fear isn't the cost of participation. It's the cost of obedience. You obey out of survival. You comply because stepping out of line feels dangerous. Not metaphorically—materially. You know exactly what's at stake if you stop playing the game. You've seen what happens when people fall. When someone misses one too many paychecks. When illness strikes without insurance. When rent goes unpaid. You know how quickly life unravels when the system decides it's done with you.

But you're never allowed to admit that you live in fear. That would disrupt the fantasy.

Instead, you're told that the system is "resilient," "complex," "ever-evolving." They speak in terms that blur meaning, using language to turn exploitation into strategy. They call it economic growth. But what grows? Not peace. Not rest. Not fulfillment. What grows is your desperation. Your dependency. Your fear of losing ground you never really owned.

The manipulation isn't just economic. It's psychological. You are bombarded with messaging designed to make you feel individually responsible for systemic conditions. Can't afford rent? Budget better. Can't pay tuition? Take out a loan. Can't keep up with bills? Pick up a second job. Every problem has a solution that blames you. Not the landlord. Not the government. Not the market. You.

And so you internalize the idea that your fear is your fault. That your financial fragility is personal. That your anxiety is something to manage alone. They isolate you in your suffering because fear loses power when it's shared out loud. Fear only thrives in silence.

That's why we don't talk about it. Not really. Not in the break room. Not in your family. Not in friend circles. You tell people you're "just tired." You say, "It's been a busy week." You say, "I'm fine." But you're not fine. You're afraid. Constantly. And somewhere deep down, you suspect the system was built to keep it that way.

You're right.

Look at the job market. You're told to be grateful for underpaid roles with no benefits. You're told to compete with people who'd do it for less. You're encouraged to settle, to silence your intuition, to say yes when your whole body is screaming no. Because saying no is risky. And risk is framed as recklessness.

Look at the banking system. It punishes you for being poor. The less you have, the more fees you pay. They sell you credit and trap you in cycles of dependence. Then they judge you for using it.

Look at housing. Rent rises faster than wages. Owning is sold as security, but you're mortgaged into a lifetime of debt. And still, any stability you achieve feels fragile. One missed payment, one job loss, one crisis—and you're back on the edge.

These aren't malfunctions. These are strategies.

The market isn't broken. It's working exactly as intended—for those it was designed to serve.

You're not meant to feel secure. You're meant to feel just secure enough. Enough to keep going. Not enough to question why. Not enough to stop. Not enough to see that the ladder you're climbing leads to a roof with no railing and no exit.

And the fear doesn't end when you "make it." If anything, it tightens. You start fearing loss. You fear falling from the rung you fought so hard to reach. You accumulate, not out of joy, but out of panic. You stockpile achievements like sandbags before a storm. But the storm never comes. It doesn't need to. Because your life has been built around preparing for it.

This is what fear-as-design looks like: an entire existence structured around avoiding catastrophe rather than pursuing meaning.

And when people crack, when they collapse under the weight of it, the system doesn't take responsibility. It blames them. As if burnout is a personal failure. As if anxiety is a character flaw. As if struggling in a hostile economic environment is a sign you just didn't try hard enough.

But what if your burnout is evidence that you're awake?

What if your exhaustion is proof that your body is rejecting the lie?

What if the fear you feel isn't yours at all—but something installed in you, programmed to keep you in your lane?

You were never meant to feel like this every day.

You weren't made to calculate survival like a spreadsheet. You weren't built to live in constant anticipation of collapse. That's not resilience. That's bondage.

And yet, here you are. Navigating a world that profits from your unease. A world that calls this "freedom" while tightening the screws.

But there is power in naming it. There is power in knowing that your anxiety isn't a personal defect—it's a political outcome. It's a design feature.

Once you name it, you can choose differently. Not immediately. Not dramatically. But internally.

You can begin to divest from the culture of fear.

You can begin to notice when you're being manipulated by headlines, by employers, by scarcity myths. You can pause before making a decision and ask, "Is this coming from alignment or anxiety?" You can stop shaming yourself for reacting to a system built to keep you unwell.

Fear only controls you when it stays invisible. So make it visible.

Trace it. Name it. Speak it out loud. Talk about it with people who are also afraid. Unmask it. Not as something broken inside you—but as something enforced around you.

Because once you see the architecture, you stop blaming the furniture.

And once you see the system for what it is, you stop worshiping its version of safety.

THE ILLUSION OF CHOICE

They told you life was about choices. That's the story. That's the hook.

They said you could be anything. Do anything. Go anywhere. They told you freedom was yours—as long as you were willing to work for it. That's how they made you believe you were in control. But they never said the menu was fixed. That every option they gave you was already filtered through fear.

You thought you were choosing. But you were only choosing between cages.

It doesn't feel like that at first. It feels like independence. You pick your career. You pick your major. You pick your city, your apartment, your credit card provider. You pick your wardrobe, your car, your phone plan. But none of these choices are free when they come pre-loaded with consequences designed to keep you small.

You're not deciding from a place of vision. You're deciding from a place of pressure. Debt pressure. Family pressure. Social pressure. The pressure to survive. The pressure to not end up on the street. The pressure to not look like a failure. These aren't decisions. These are panic responses dressed up in LinkedIn language.

You didn't pick your job because it lit you up. You picked it because you couldn't afford to wait. You didn't move to that city because it felt like home. You moved because the rent was cheaper. You didn't major in that field because you were passionate. You did it because someone convinced you it was "practical." Almost every move you've made, every box you've checked, every so-called step forward in your adult life was filtered through one question: *what will hurt the least?*

That's not choice. That's damage control.

But no one admits that. Because to admit it would mean admitting that freedom, as we've been sold, is a costume. It would mean facing the terrifying truth that most of your life has been guided not by desire, but by **fear management**. And that truth is too much for most people. So we keep playing the game. We keep celebrating decisions that are really just evasions.

Go to school or be irrelevant. Take the promotion or be left behind. Buy a house or be seen as unstable. Start a family or be labeled selfish.

Every one of these choices carries a consequence prepackaged by cultural expectation and economic conditioning. You don't get to say no without risk. You don't get to deviate without cost. You're not free to choose—you're free to conform in a slightly different color.

Look at the job market. The gig economy is branded as flexibility. Freelancing is sold as autonomy. But beneath the branding is desperation. People aren't freelancing because it's liberating. They're doing it because the system has made traditional employment so unstable, so underpaid, so soul-crushing that going solo feels like the lesser evil. That's not choice. That's the illusion of escape from a burning building you never set on fire.

Even your rebellion is prepackaged.

They've monetized it. Co-opted it. Given it an aesthetic and sold it back to you. You think you're subverting the system by quitting your 9-to-5, starting a side hustle, chasing a "laptop lifestyle." But the architecture hasn't changed. You're still trapped in productivity metrics. You're still operating under performance anxiety. You're still building your identity on deliverables.

You might not have a boss. But you still have fear.

This is how deep the illusion runs.

You were told that every option was available. But availability means nothing if every path is paved with conditions. If every exit is lined with consequence. They call it freedom, but it's freedom with a leash. You can move—but only as far as your debt-to-income ratio allows. You can speak—but only if you keep your job. You can choose—but only from what they've already decided is acceptable.

Even the way you dream has been infiltrated.

You've stopped dreaming based on what you actually want. You now dream based on what feels possible inside a fear-based system. You dream within brackets. You scale down your ambitions to make them more "realistic." You shape your vision around what won't upset the balance, what won't threaten your income, what won't shake your relationships, what won't risk your image.

And you tell yourself it's maturity.

But it's not.

It's surrender.

When every decision you make is weighed against potential collapse, you are not living. You are **curating an illusion of stability**. You are micromanaging your own life like it's a public relations campaign. You are playing defense against a world you believe is out to break you—and maybe you're right.

That belief didn't come from nowhere.

It came from watching people you love lose everything. It came from seeing the wrong turn one generation took and swearing you'd never repeat it. It came from being punished the last time you chose something bold. It came from learning that safety isn't granted—it's negotiated. And the price is always your authenticity.

So you build a life you can tolerate.

One that looks successful.

One that others respect.

One that allows you to sleep—lightly.

But that's not freedom. That's strategy. And eventually, strategy will rot your soul.

You will wake up one day in a life that looks good on paper and feel like a stranger in your own skin. You will realize you were so busy trying not to fall apart that you never figured out what wholeness actually means.

And the scariest part?

You won't know how to get it back.

Because there is no map for reclaiming desire when you've spent your life navigating fear. There is no GPS for reimagining choice when all you've known is limitation. You have to build that compass yourself.

And it starts with interrogation.

Every choice you've made—put it on trial. Not with judgment. But with curiosity. Ask yourself: *Was this my truth, or my survival instinct? Did I pick this because I wanted it, or because I feared the alternative? Who was I trying to protect? Who was I trying to impress? What part of me did I silence to make this work?*

You may not like the answers.

But they will set you free.

Because once you see the structure, you don't fall for the story.

And when you stop falling for the story, you begin to reclaim your choices—not the ones the system gave you, but the ones you buried. The ones that made no sense on paper but whispered to your soul.

The ones you pushed away because they didn't look profitable, logical, or scalable. The ones that didn't fit neatly into five-year plans or personal branding statements. The ones that felt risky—until you realized risk was the only real freedom you ever had.

This reclamation is not fast. It's not clean. And it's not comfortable.

But it's real.

It begins with small acts of defiance. Saying no when fear says yes. Saying yes when logic says no. Choosing alignment over optics. Choosing rest over progress. Choosing quiet over performance. Choosing truth over comfort.

It's not about burning your life down. It's about peeling away the parts that were never yours to begin with.

And you'll know the difference.

Because what's yours feels like relief.

And what's not feels like a checklist.

So no, you haven't been free.

But you're not powerless either.

You can start now. Not by changing your entire life overnight, but by seeing it clearly. By removing the mask that says "this is what I wanted" and exposing the layers of compromise beneath. By calling out the fear. Not as a flaw—but as the architect.

You don't owe anyone your compliance. You don't owe the system your loyalty. You don't owe the past your continued obedience.

What you owe yourself is this: to choose like you're free, even if you're still afraid.

Because that's where real power begins.

"You weren't chasing freedom – you were chasing a stable prison cell."

GENERATIONAL OBEDIENCE

You didn't invent your fear. You inherited it.

Long before you made your first paycheck, long before you opened your first bank account, long before you ever felt the sickening drop of an empty wallet, that fear was already waiting for you—wrapped in your father's eyes, coded in your mother's voice, embedded in your family's dinner conversations.

It came in stories, in warnings, in advice disguised as love.

"Get a real job."

"Don't take chances."

"Security first."

"Be grateful you even have work."

These weren't just phrases. They were commandments. Not because your parents didn't love you, but because fear taught them that love had to sound like caution. Because they learned the hard way that to survive, you had to play it safe. And then they taught you to survive the same way.

It didn't feel like fear at the time. It felt like wisdom. It felt like maturity. It felt like responsibility. But it was fear all along—dressed up in Sunday clothes, passed down like sacred scripture.

You were handed a script written in survival language. A generational playbook where the best move was always the least risky one. Where the highest achievement was a steady paycheck. Where success wasn't freedom—it was consistency. Predictability. Compliance.

Your life started with borrowed beliefs.

And those beliefs didn't come from nowhere. They came from systems built to condition entire generations into submission. School didn't teach you how to question power. It taught you how to raise your hand, how to line up, how to follow rules written by people you would never meet. It taught you that performance mattered more than purpose, and that memorization would be rewarded more than imagination.

You weren't educated—you were **domesticated**.

You learned to sit still, to ask for permission, to suppress impulse, to internalize judgment. You were told that risk equals recklessness and that passion was optional unless it paid. By the time you graduated, you had mastered obedience without even realizing it.

And it didn't stop there.

The institutions you entered—jobs, governments, universities, corporations—continued the training. They refined it. They specialized it. They gave it polish. Obedience wasn't just encouraged—it was incentivized. The less you questioned, the more stable you became. The more you conformed, the more praise you received. And any time you started to drift toward curiosity, doubt, rebellion—they pulled you back with fear.

"Think about your future."

"Don't throw it all away."

"You're lucky to be here."

So you learned to nod. You learned to suppress. You learned to stay in rooms you hated because they came with benefits. You learned to say "I'm fine" while dying inside. And eventually, you stopped noticing the dissonance.

You called it adulthood. But really, it was indoctrination.

Obedience became identity.

And the tragedy is, you weren't the first. Your parents went through it. Their parents before them. Entire generations trained not to dream too big, not to risk too much, not to speak too loud. Because at some point, they were punished for trying.

They tried to start a business—and failed.

They tried to chase art—and went broke.

They tried to stand up—and got crushed.

They tried to do things differently—and were labeled irresponsible, ungrateful, naive.

And so they built a worldview where failure was more dangerous than regret. Where risk was something only the privileged could afford. Where deviation wasn't courage—it was betrayal.

And now, here you are. Still paying the price for someone else's trauma.

You didn't just inherit your family's name or history. You inherited their emotional architecture. Their caution. Their beliefs about what's possible, what's smart, what's allowed.

You didn't come into this world afraid of being poor. You learned it from stories. You learned it from watching your parents flinch every time the bank called. You learned it from hearing how they stayed in jobs they hated "for the sake of the kids." You learned it from watching them equate sacrifice with morality.

This is how fear becomes culture.

It becomes tradition. It becomes a badge of honor to suffer quietly. To sacrifice endlessly. To play it safe and call it love. And then it becomes a crime to want more. Not just more money— but more **life**. More truth. More expression. More ownership of your time, your voice, your energy.

Wanting more becomes selfish. And rebellion becomes betrayal.

This is how institutions keep winning. Not by force—but by inheritance. They don't need to chain you. Your parents already did that. With good intentions. With exhausted hearts. With tired hands and trembling voices. They passed down their fears thinking they were giving you protection.

But fear is not protection.

It's preservation. And preservation is not the same as liberation.

You cannot build a free life using tools designed to survive captivity.

And until you understand that, you will mistake your cage for a safety net.

You'll keep walking the same roads, checking the same boxes, chasing the same praise. You'll call it stability. You'll call it being grounded. But what it really is—is generational obedience masquerading as wisdom.

Obedience is seductive because it's socially rewarded. Obedience keeps you likable. It keeps you in the will. It keeps you at the dinner table. It keeps you from making others uncomfortable.

Because the moment you start asking real questions, the room gets quiet.

"Why should I stay at a job that makes me sick?"

"Why can't I live with less and have more peace?"

"What if the thing I want doesn't make sense on paper?"

"What if I don't want the life everyone else wants?"

These questions make people squirm. Because they force reflection. They force honesty. They threaten the fragile identities built on sacrifice.

And most people would rather shame you than question themselves.

So they dismiss you. They say you're irresponsible, idealistic, ungrateful. They use shame to pull you back into the script. And if shame doesn't work, they use guilt.

They remind you how hard they worked.

How much they sacrificed.

How lucky you are.

How easy you have it.

But their pain doesn't make your truth any less valid.

Their survival doesn't mean you must abandon your liberation.

You can honor where they came from without staying stuck there.

You can love them—and still leave the cage they built.

This is what breaking the cycle looks like. It's not glamorous. It's not always loud. It doesn't always come with applause.

Sometimes, it's just sitting with your choices and realizing most of them weren't yours. Sometimes, it's grieving the life you thought was secure—but was only ever safe for who you used to be.

The truth is, every generation is offered a choice.

Continue the pattern. Or disrupt it.

And disruption is terrifying. It comes with loss. It comes with misunderstanding. It comes with exile from the comfort of being seen as "one of us." But it also comes with the one thing your ancestors never had enough of: **freedom of expression**.

You don't have to perpetuate their fear. You don't have to preserve their struggle. You don't have to inherit their limitation and call it legacy.

You can bless their survival.

And still reject their obedience.

You can create a life that's no longer rooted in defense.

Because at some point, someone has to stop the echo. Someone has to interrupt the inheritance. Someone has to say, "I refuse to keep living like this just because everyone else did."

That someone is you.

You can be the break in the line. You can be the quiet revolution in your family tree. You can be the first one who chose love over fear, truth over tradition, possibility over programming.

You don't owe fear your loyalty just because it kept them alive.

Your task is not to mimic their path.

Your task is to become the kind of ancestor that future generations won't have to heal from.

That begins the moment you stop mistaking caution for character.

You were not born to repeat history. You were born to remake it.

BREAKING THE FEAR CONTRACT

At some point in your life, you signed a contract you don't remember signing. It wasn't written in ink. It didn't have a signature. But you agreed to it anyway. You agreed to stay small in exchange for protection. You agreed to trade your edge for stability. You agreed to silence your instincts so you could be seen as smart, reliable, grounded. You didn't know it then, but what you signed was a **fear contract**—an unspoken agreement to live within the lines in exchange for the illusion of security.

You agreed to jobs that didn't fit, to hours that drained you, to silence that suffocated. You agreed to the 40-year plan, the benefits package, the muted grief that came with shelving your real desires. You agreed to the hierarchy. You agreed to the scripts. And each time you wanted out, you reminded yourself that freedom was too dangerous, too uncertain, too reckless. So you stayed. And you called it responsibility.

But here's what they didn't tell you when you signed that contract: the safety you were promised doesn't exist. Not in the way they sold it. Not in the form of job titles, salary brackets, or long-term plans. Because the economy isn't built on protection. It's built on pressure. And the longer you follow the rules, the more you realize the rules were never designed to lead you anywhere real. They were written to keep you predictable.

You were raised to fear risk, but what you were never told is that risk is not the enemy—numbness is. Risk makes you alert. Risk keeps you connected to what's alive in you. Risk requires honesty. Numbness, on the other hand, lets you rot slowly in the name of being sensible. And that rot is what's been eating at you for years.

The fear contract doesn't just limit your choices. It limits your **identity**. You start to confuse stability with personality. You start to mistake predictability for virtue. You lose sight of the fact that most of your decisions haven't come from alignment—they've come from calculation. Not because you're weak. But because that's how you were trained.

You were trained to think five steps ahead. To anticipate disaster. To obsess over fallback plans. To abandon the present moment in the name of future control. You were taught that the worst thing that could happen was being unprepared. But the real tragedy isn't being unprepared—it's being unchanged. It's building a life so guarded that you never experience yourself outside the metrics of survival.

There's a moment in every adult life when you realize the thing you thought would make you safe has only made you smaller. For some, that moment comes during burnout. For others, it's a sudden loss—a job, a person, a future. But it's in that collapse that the truth becomes impossible to ignore: the safety you built is brittle. And all that fear you obeyed never bought you the peace you were promised.

That's when the contract starts to feel heavy.

It doesn't break all at once. It frays. It creaks. It starts to split in subtle ways. You get tired of justifying decisions you don't believe in. You resent the version of yourself you had to become to keep the peace. You feel moments of defiance. Tiny surges of rebellion. And if you're paying attention, you begin to wonder what it might feel like to tear it all up.

But then the old voice returns. The one that says, "What if you lose everything?" It tells you to wait. To be grateful. To play it safe for a little longer. It reminds you of all the people who stayed quiet and were rewarded. It reminds you that risk is for the privileged, for the reckless, for the naive.

That voice isn't yours. It's the voice of a system afraid of what happens when you start choosing differently. Because the moment you choose truth over fear, you become unmanageable.

To break the fear contract is not to become reckless. It's to become sovereign. It's not about quitting everything, burning it all down, or becoming a martyr for authenticity. It's about choosing from a place of truth instead of trauma. It's about no longer saying yes when your entire body says no. It's about noticing when your decisions are being hijacked by imagined disaster instead of lived alignment.

You don't need to gamble everything to choose risk. You need to stop pretending that risk is optional. Because living is inherently risky. Every form of growth requires it. Every moment of aliveness demands it. You're already risking your peace by staying where you are. The only question is whether the risk you're taking leads to expansion or just extends the performance.

People often talk about financial risk as if it's the only risk that matters. But there are other forms of loss that cost more. The risk of self-betrayal. The risk of wasting years doing something you never loved. The risk of looking back and realizing you were always waiting for permission that never came.

Security is not the opposite of risk. It's the reward of self-trust. When you know yourself, when you honor what you know to be true, when you stop outsourcing your value to external systems, you become dangerous. Not in the chaotic sense. But in the sense that no one can hold your fear hostage anymore. And that kind of inner security is the only thing that lasts.

This isn't about fearlessness. That's a myth. You don't need to be fearless to live honestly. You need to be willing to move with fear, not for it. Fear will always be there, whispering worst-case scenarios, forecasting your collapse, warning you about what might go wrong. But fear isn't prophecy. It's programming. And you don't have to obey it.

You can learn to listen without submission. You can acknowledge the voice without letting it dictate your movements. You can feel afraid and still choose the thing that sets you free.

But this takes practice. And most importantly, it takes **grief**.

Grief for the years spent playing it safe. Grief for the versions of you that went quiet to keep the peace. Grief for the opportunities lost to hesitation. Grief for the people you became to survive. This grief is holy. It is not a step backward. It is not weakness. It is the cost of awakening.

You've spent your life trying to outrun fear. Trying to out-plan it, outwork it, out-earn it. But fear can't be conquered. It can only be witnessed. You have to turn around and face it. Look it in the eye and ask: "What are you really protecting me from?" You'll find that it's not death, or loss, or ruin. It's shame. It's rejection. It's being seen in your rawest truth and not being validated.

And once you know that, you can start validating yourself.

This is what breaking the contract looks like: choosing self-trust over safety. Choosing risk in service of alignment. Choosing not to be defined by your most frightened voice.

It might be messy. It might be misunderstood. You might lose things. Relationships. Comfort. Familiarity. But you will gain something else. Something no contract can ever guarantee: yourself.

And once you've tasted that, you will never sell your soul for security again.

"You weren't avoiding failure. You were avoiding freedom because it didn't come with guarantees."

REFLECTION QUESTIONS

- Is the security you're chasing real—or is it just a story designed to keep you obedient?
- Who benefits from your fear of financial instability— and who would you be without that fear?
- How many of your life choices were truly free—and how many were made under financial pressure disguised as "responsibility"?
- Do you equate stability with submission? If so, when did safety become a prison?
- What illusions have you inherited about success, safety, and scarcity—and are you brave enough to let them die?

CHAPTER FIVE
THE SYSTEM'S MASTERPLAN

"You were never poor – you were just priced out of someone else's idea of value."

CURRENCY AND CONTROL

You were told money was just a tool. Neutral. Objective. A means of exchange. That's the most dangerous lie you've ever believed. Because the moment you accepted that idea, you stopped questioning who designed the tool, who profits from its use, and who gets punished when they don't play along.

Money was never neutral. It was born to **govern behavior**.

At its core, it doesn't just buy things—it decides things. Where you live. What you eat. Who listens when you speak. Who waits when you walk into a room. Who works for whom. And more importantly, who never gets to say no.

The system doesn't control you with fear. It controls you with currency. It wraps control in the illusion of opportunity. You're told you're free to make choices, but every choice is measured against what you can afford. The house you live in. The shoes your kid wears to school. The food you're able to feed your aging parents. The moment money enters the equation, autonomy leaves.

You're not told what to do with your life. But if you don't trade time for money, you starve. That's not freedom. That's **coercion in a tuxedo**.

Look at how it plays out.

A man wakes up in a city he can barely afford. He works twelve hours a day at a job that makes his spine ache and his soul go silent. He hates it. But every time he considers quitting, he remembers the rent. The kids. The medical bills. The unspoken shame of failure. So he shrinks his rebellion. He shows up again the next day.

A woman drags herself to a job interview for a role she knows she's overqualified for. She's polite. Grateful. Obedient. She lowers her salary expectations before they even ask, just to appear cooperative. Not because she lacks confidence—but because she's six months behind on car payments and her account balance is the only thing screaming louder than her instincts.

A university student wants to pursue anthropology, or literature, or design. But their family "reminds" them that those degrees don't pay. So they default to business or engineering. Not because they want to —but because they've internalized the idea that a paycheck matters more than purpose. They spend four years in classes they can't stand, praying the diploma buys them enough future to afford joy later.

This is how control works now. Not with violence, but with calculations. You're not beaten into obedience—you calculate your way into it. And every part of the system is built to make sure those calculations feel justified.

You're taught to see money as freedom. But freedom that disappears the moment your job does? That's not freedom. That's a rental agreement.

What you really have is a permission slip. Signed by your paycheck. Valid only as long as you keep performing.

And yet, the system parades this as success. You're praised for waking up at 5am to go to a job that quietly kills your health. You're applauded for "doing what you have to do" to make ends meet. You're told to be proud of your struggle—as if it's a virtue, not a trap.

Look at how normalized dependency has become.

Your healthcare is tied to your employer. Your visa, your benefits, your access to decent housing—they all hinge on your ability to serve the machine. One misstep, one injury, one moment of burnout—and the scaffolding of your life crumbles. And when it does, they tell you it's your fault. That you should've planned better. Saved better. Worked harder.

The system profits from your permanent **anxiety**. It needs you in motion—always chasing, never arriving.

Because the moment you feel stable, you might stop. And if you stop, you might think. And if you think, you might start asking questions.

So the system feeds you just enough to survive, never enough to rest.

It looks like opportunity. It smells like choice. But if you scratch beneath the surface, it's just behavioral engineering. You are being conditioned every day to associate money with morality, struggle with strength, and survival with success.

Why do you think the worst insult in society is being called "lazy"? Not "cruel." Not "dishonest." Lazy. Because laziness implies disconnection from the machine. A refusal to produce. A lack of usefulness to the economy. We don't value humanity—we value productivity. And we've wrapped that productivity in the language of virtue.

You're not judged by how well you love. You're judged by how much you earn.

A man who works 80 hours a week but can't name his child's teacher is seen as disciplined. A woman who chooses part-time work to care for her dying parent is seen as unserious. A family that downsizes to reclaim their peace is asked, "Are you okay financially?"

We don't care about people. We care about performance.

You might think this doesn't apply to you because you have choices. But how many of your choices are fear-based? You pay into systems you don't believe in because you're scared of what happens if you don't. You accept job offers that feel wrong in your gut because you've convinced yourself it's "just temporary." You stay in careers you resent because you're terrified of not being able to pay for the life that proves you're successful.

Money isn't the problem. It's the architecture around it.

Banks don't just store your income—they profile your worthiness. Your credit score doesn't reflect your character—it reflects your obedience. It punishes you for not borrowing "the right way," for not playing the game by their rules. Even your access to basic services is filtered through metrics designed to reward conformity and punish rebellion.

Try being self-employed and applying for a mortgage. Suddenly, you're a risk. A question mark. Try living outside a salary system and watch how fast society calls you unstable, even if you're thriving.

Control doesn't always look like handcuffs. Sometimes, it looks like paperwork.

It looks like standing in line at a government office, trying to prove your right to assistance. It looks like waiting on hold with customer service, begging for a refund you can't afford to lose. It looks like making polite small talk with a manager you despise, just to avoid rocking the boat.

It's death by compliance. And you're expected to be grateful for it.

Because at least you're not homeless. At least you have food. At least you're employed.

That's how low the bar is.

Control is maintained through fear-based gratitude. Be thankful, or lose everything. Stay quiet, or start over. Obey, or get labeled difficult, delusional, ungrateful.

And what does this cost you?

It costs you your voice.

It costs you your timing.

It costs you the right to pause.

To reflect.

To change direction without being penalized.

You weren't built for this. Your biology didn't evolve for spreadsheets and marketing funnels. But the system doesn't care about biology. It only cares about inputs and outputs.

You're not a person—you're an asset.

And once you stop being profitable, they'll replace you.

That's the part no one says out loud. You're only safe as long as you're useful. And usefulness isn't measured in compassion or creativity. It's measured in revenue potential.

So yes, money matters. But not in the way you think.

Money doesn't just buy comfort. It buys proximity to control. It buys access to systems that insulate you from instability. It buys the right to say no without immediate punishment.

And that's why you're stuck.

Because you're not chasing abundance. You're chasing protection. But protection that expires the moment you fall behind? That's not real protection. That's emotional blackmail.

You didn't consent to this system.

But you're punished for questioning it.

And if you walk away, you're marked.

Try leaving the workforce to write a book, start a movement, raise your kids, or heal from burnout. Watch how fast people ask, "So... what are you doing now?" They're not curious. They're checking your alignment with the system.

The system is fragile. That's why it needs your constant participation.

And every time you question it, you reveal its cracks.

So let this be your invitation to start seeing money not as a goal— but as a control mechanism. And once you name that, you can start reclaiming power where the system least expects it:

In the refusal to perform.

In the audacity to pause.

In the quiet choice to define success by something no one can measure.

"The system didn't shackle your body – it colonized your beliefs."

FEAR-BASED ARCHITECTURE

You've been told the system is chaotic. That it's unstable. That inflation, layoffs, housing crises, and debt spirals are unfortunate side effects of a "complex" world.

But what if that instability is intentional?

What if the fear isn't a malfunction—but the engine?

You're not supposed to feel secure. You're supposed to feel just unsafe enough to stay obedient. To keep applying. To keep settling. To keep grinding. That is the architecture of this economy: invisible fear woven into every structure that touches your life.

Let's start with something simple—your job. How many people do you know who actually feel secure in their work? Not performative confidence. Real safety. The kind that lets you breathe.

Here's the answer: almost none.

In 2022, Microsoft conducted a global work trends report that showed over **40% of employees** were considering leaving their jobs, not because they were lazy or unmotivated—but because the pressure had become unbearable. Burnout, instability, and corporate gaslighting had become the baseline. But most of them stayed. Why? Because walking away meant risking everything—rent, healthcare, reputation, social status, maybe even the ability to buy groceries next week.

Even white-collar workers aren't immune. Take Patrick McKenzie, a respected software engineer and founder. In a public blog post, he recounted how after working for Stripe—a billion-dollar fintech company—he still experienced persistent financial anxiety. Despite earning a six-figure salary, he worried about leaving. Why? Because tech layoffs were hitting mid-career engineers hard, and "starting over" at 40 wasn't as simple as it sounded. The fear wasn't about being broke. It was about being disposable.

That's not freedom. That's architecture.

Fear is coded into the labor market.

Entry-level jobs now require years of experience. Gig workers are penalized for taking sick days. Warehouse workers wear wrist monitors to track movement—treated more like robots than people. Freelancers are praised for "owning their careers," but they live without benefits, without stable income, without legal protection.

You're told to hustle. But the moment you stop—just to breathe—there's a consequence. That consequence isn't just financial. It's emotional. You start questioning your worth. Because in this architecture, value is measured in urgency.

We're not talking about laziness versus ambition. That's a false binary created by the system to keep the pressure on. This isn't about work ethic. It's about how deeply your survival has been tied to manufactured fear.

The system punishes pause.

Try taking a sabbatical without being seen as "drifting." Try spending a year caring for an ill parent and reentering the workforce without being asked to explain the "gap." Try downsizing your lifestyle and notice how people look at you differently. We don't reward sustainability. We reward stress.

This isn't accidental. It's economically engineered.

Take inflation. You're told it's a normal fluctuation. But in many countries, inflation far outpaces wage growth. That's not natural. That's a systemic theft of purchasing power, silently squeezing you while CEO bonuses break records. It's not a crisis. It's a transfer.

Even the housing market is designed to trap. Mortgages stretch 30+ years—lifelong obedience contracts disguised as "investments." Renters face annual hikes while wages stagnate. Fear of eviction becomes a behavioral tool: don't protest, don't miss work, don't fall out of line.

Fear is also coded into digital systems.

In China, the government's Social Credit System gives citizens a numerical trustworthiness score. Late payments or criticizing authority can limit your ability to buy train tickets, travel abroad, or qualify for loans. In the West, it's less visible—but it exists. Miss a credit card payment, and your score drops. Try renting an apartment with a low score. Try getting a business loan.

Suddenly, you're locked out—not because you're incapable, but because the system flagged you as risky.

You are always being monitored, rated, and scored.

But here's the kicker: it's not about stopping you from failing. It's about keeping you scared enough not to try something different.

Ask any immigrant family. The pressure to "make it" is rarely just about comfort. It's about *not losing everything*. It's about being one step ahead of disaster. It's about being able to say yes to your landlord, your employer, your government—so that they never question your place in the system.

And the closer you get to comfort, the more afraid you become of losing it. You finally get the stable job, and suddenly you're terrified of being laid off. You finally buy the house, and now you're tied to 30 years of "safe choices." You finally have health insurance—but only if you stay employed. Comfort comes with a choke chain.

This isn't conspiracy. It's behavioral economics.

Design a system that keeps people afraid to stop working, and you don't need to govern them by force. They'll govern themselves. They'll overwork, self-censor, settle, and justify it all as "being practical." And every now and then, the system rewards a few outliers—just enough to give everyone else hope that maybe, if they just grind harder, they'll be next.

The architecture of fear doesn't just live in banks and policies—it lives in us.

In the way we shame ourselves for resting. In the guilt we feel for saying no. In the fear we carry when we think about taking risks. In the voice that says, "You can't afford to mess this up." That voice was placed there by design.

And what does it cost?

It costs peace. Joy. Presence. Sanity. Your ability to daydream without a budget spreadsheet. Your ability to make decisions based on truth, not trauma. Your ability to choose alignment instead of affordability.

Most people don't fear being broke. They fear being blamed for being broke. They fear what poverty says about their worth. Because in a fear-based economy, having less is treated like a character flaw. You're told you must've done something wrong. You weren't smart enough, strategic enough, disciplined enough.

But here's the truth: in a fear-designed world, doing everything "right" still isn't enough.

You could get the degree, follow the plan, show up on time, play the game—and still lose. Because the architecture was never built to support you. It was built to extract you.

And when you break down? When anxiety takes over? When the burnout becomes unbearable?

You're prescribed therapy. Medication. Resilience training.

You're told to fix yourself.

Not the system.

DEPENDENCE AS DESIGN

You weren't meant to escape. That's the secret most people don't find out until it's too late.

Everything around you—every contract, every payment plan, every "convenience"—was built not to liberate you, but to bind you. Not with chains. With timelines. Penalties. Interest rates.

Fine print. Dependency isn't a consequence of poverty. It's the goal of the system. They want you functional—but never fully free.

Let's stop pretending this is about financial literacy. This isn't about whether you understand budgeting, or whether you read the loan terms before signing. It's about how every option you're given—education, housing, credit, work—is pre-loaded with hooks designed to keep you tethered.

Take education.

You're told that college is the gateway to opportunity. That if you want options, upward mobility, and dignity, you need a degree. But what they don't tell you is that for most students, that degree will cost decades of repayment and compound interest. In the U.S., **student loan debt has passed $1.7 trillion**. That's not a policy oversight. That's a business model.

You graduate with a piece of paper and a financial leash. That debt shapes your entire adult life. You take the job that pays fastest, not the one that fits best. You delay travel, risk, exploration. You say no to internships that could have opened doors—because they don't pay. You avoid career pivots because your payments don't pause. You don't move cities. You don't start that business. Not because you can't dream—but because you can't afford to.

You aren't free to build.

You're locked into repaying.

And when you finally pay it off—years, sometimes decades later—do you feel empowered? Or just relieved that you finally get to start living on your terms?

That's not liberation. That's delayed permission.

Now look at housing. Owning a home is painted as the gold standard of success. A sign of adulthood, stability, and arrival. But underneath the glossy brochures, there's a trap.

Mortgages are structured dependency. You "own" your home— but only if you continue to pay for 20 to 35 years. Miss a few payments, and the house isn't yours anymore. And those payments? They include interest stacked so high, you often pay double the actual value of the home by the time you're done.

And what about renters? They're worse off—trapped in the illusion of freedom, while every renewal notice comes with a higher price tag and a reminder that they could be displaced at any moment.

Housing is not security. It's conditional shelter.

The same goes for healthcare. In many countries, the ability to receive basic medical care is tied directly to your job. If you leave or get laid off, you don't just lose income—you lose your right to stay healthy. How can you make empowered choices when your next doctor visit depends on an HR department you despise?

Dependency is not a side effect of being poor. It's a built-in feature of economic life—even for the middle class.

Credit cards make it worse. They offer flexibility on the front end and silent extraction on the back. Interest rates that climb into double digits. Late fees that appear like digital ghosts. You buy a $300 emergency flight, and if you can't pay it off that month, you may end up paying $800 for the same trip. That isn't a financial tool. That's debt as a long-game trap.

Even conveniences are layered with dependency.

Subscriptions that auto-renew. Buy-now-pay-later schemes that encourage spending beyond your means. App ecosystems that require monthly access fees just to stay competitive in your career. You don't even own your software anymore—you rent the tools that let you earn a living.

Try cancelling. Try simplifying. Try stepping outside the grid. And you'll see just how deeply embedded the design is.

Even transportation is rigged.

In most urban centers, car ownership isn't a luxury—it's a requirement. Public infrastructure is underfunded. Walkability is limited. If you don't drive, your employability drops. But cars are just another form of indentured mobility. Down payments. Insurance premiums. Repairs. Fuel. Interest on car loans. Parking tickets. Tolls. Owning a vehicle often means permanent partial debt. You're mobile—but never financially still.

And just in case you try to escape the system through entrepreneurship—there's a trap for that too.

Start a business? Great. Now pay taxes every quarter. Pay for your own health insurance. Manage unpredictable income cycles. Compete against VC-backed tech giants who can underprice you out of existence. Build an audience online? Now you're subject to platform rules, shadowbans, algorithm shifts, and terms of service you never agreed to.

You're never really sovereign. You're just picking which dependency you want to serve.

Here's what makes this worse than traditional control: It all feels like your idea.

You chose the college.

You signed the lease. You started the business.

You applied for the card.

You clicked "subscribe."

That's the genius of modern capitalism. It packages dependency as autonomy. It turns lifelong debt into "investment." It turns necessity into "flexibility." You believe you're self-made, but the only thing you've made is a life built on financial commitments you can't walk away from without consequences.

Even digital life now enforces economic dependence. Want to be relevant in your field? You need access to paid learning platforms. Want to stay visible? You need marketing software. Want to sell something? Pay for Stripe, PayPal, Shopify, social ads. Want your content to be seen? Boost it. Promote it. Monetize it. The attention economy doesn't reward creativity—it rewards the ability to afford the tools of visibility.

That's why it's not enough to work hard anymore. You also have to pay to compete.

So you work to earn, just to pay to be seen, just to maybe earn more.

It's a closed loop.

Dependency wasn't designed to look oppressive. It was designed to look like the only way to live.

Look around. You'll see it everywhere.

- A mother returns to work 12 weeks postpartum—not because she wants to, but because unpaid maternity leave doesn't feed her baby.
- A software engineer sticks with a toxic startup for two years because leaving means losing their green card.
- A teacher with a chronic illness drags herself into school

every morning, because without full-time hours, she loses her health benefits.

- A single man nearing 60 keeps working soul-crushing night shifts, because his mortgage has 8 years left—and if he downsizes now, he loses everything he's built.

These are not failures. These are the expected outcomes of a world designed to keep you leveraged. Every system is structured like a casino: the house always wins. The goal isn't to destroy you. The goal is to keep you playing. As long as you keep spinning the wheel, feeding the machine, you're valuable.

But the moment you unplug?

You're a liability.

So they build in fear. Scarcity. Reputational shame. They teach you that stepping off the grid is irresponsible. They call minimalism lazy. They call slowness weakness. They call disconnection failure.

And because the system is so deeply embedded in your relationships, even the people who love you will try to pull you back in.

"Are you sure you want to quit that job?"

"Is this really the right time to say no to a promotion?"

"You're going to cancel your health insurance… on purpose?"

What they're really asking is:

"How are you going to survive without the system we all depend on?"

Because that's what they've taught us to believe: That survival requires submission. That maturity means long-term debt. That success means being too busy to rest.

But what if that's the real scam?

What if maturity isn't about signing 30-year contracts, but about asking better questions?

What if real adulthood means learning how to live without being owned?

What if success isn't having more options—but needing fewer?

That's what the system fears most:

Not failure.

But the day you no longer need it to feel whole.

"They didn't need to chain you – they just taught you to fear freedom."

THE ILLUSION OF PROGRESS

You were never promised freedom. You were promised progress.

Not the kind that liberates you. The kind that makes you think you're moving forward while you're running in place.

The modern system doesn't need you starving. That would cause rebellion. It just needs you slightly satisfied—fed enough to keep hoping, but controlled enough to never stop obeying. This is how dependency sustains itself: by offering rewards at perfectly timed intervals to keep you chasing what you'll never truly catch.

It's the behavioral logic of a casino, disguised as economics.

You push a button. Sometimes you win. Mostly you don't. But every now and then, the machine gives you just enough to keep you believing. A raise. A tax refund. A promotion that comes with a bigger title but the same stress. And each time, you feel like you're almost there. Close. Just a little more. Just one more project. One more year. One more sale. One more sacrifice.

And so, you stay.

Not because it's working.

But because you're emotionally invested in the story that it might someday work.

The system doesn't thrive on your failure. It thrives on your almost.

It rewards you just enough to numb your questions. Not enough to quit the chase.

Look at corporate promotion cycles. You're told to prove yourself, hit your KPIs, show initiative. Then you're moved up one level. New title. Maybe 8% more pay. But what they don't tell you is that the responsibilities double and the expectations triple. The reward is not mobility—it's deeper entanglement.

And you say yes. Because it's the "next step." Because you've already given so much that turning back feels like wasting your past.

That's the trap. **Sunk cost disguised as success.**

You're not climbing a ladder. You're running on a treadmill someone else controls.

Now look at consumption cycles.

Have you ever noticed how quickly joy fades after a purchase? That sense of arrival you feel when you upgrade your phone, your car, your wardrobe—how fast does it disappear? You chase dopamine in the form of delivery boxes and swipeable upgrades. The system knows you need to feel progress, so it offers it in 2-day shipping.

But the feeling doesn't last. It's not designed to. Because lasting satisfaction would break the loop.

You think you're building a life. But what you're really building is **a tolerance to the illusion of reward**.

Each step forward gives you just enough to keep investing. But never enough to disengage.

Even government systems are structured this way. Look at tax incentives, subsidies, social assistance. They're offered as support —but only to those who keep following the script. Earn too little, you're penalized. Earn too much, you're disqualified. The sweet spot? Be dependent just enough to need help, but not enough to challenge the system offering it.

Even personal finance culture plays this game.

You're told to save 20% of your income, invest in index funds, and plan for retirement. And yes, those are smart moves—on paper. But no one talks about the emotional gymnastics required to delay your life for 40 years in hopes of peace when you're 70. They call it financial literacy. But in practice, it's just behavioral patience under economic pressure.

The more you comply, the more you're rewarded with… waiting.

Waiting for one day. Waiting for the payout. Waiting for the season when everything finally feels okay.

But "one day" is a moving target. It never lands. Because the system doesn't run on fulfillment—it runs on deferral.

Now let's talk about the reward structures hidden in social life.

Think about the friend who gets celebrated for buying a house—even if it drains their savings and kills their freedom. Think about the family member praised for staying in a "good job" for 25 years, even though they hated it. Think about how people respond when you say you're "taking time to figure things out." There's a brief silence. Then a polite nod. Then the question: "So… what's next?"

Why? Because progress is the only acceptable currency of self-worth.

You're allowed to exist, as long as you're improving. As long as you're working toward something tangible. As long as you're not sitting still for too long. Stillness triggers concern. Not because it's dangerous—but because it threatens the very architecture of dependency.

Stillness is anti-system. It says, "I don't need to chase to matter."

But the system won't let that sit. So it gives you something new to chase. Always something just out of reach.

The reward for your loyalty isn't freedom. It's more structured ambition.

Even tech platforms use this logic. Instagram doesn't reward authentic connection. It rewards engagement cycles. The more often you post, the more often you're seen. The more you optimize your content, the more followers you gain. But step back for a week? You disappear.

You're rewarded with visibility—as long as you stay dependent on the platform to exist.

The same happens in academia. The more papers you publish, the more citations you get. The more citations, the more grant money. But fall behind once—take a break, shift careers, pause to raise a child—and you're irrelevant. You're not valued for your thinking. You're valued for your output consistency.

This isn't about production. It's about behavioral loyalty.

They keep you hoping. Not thriving.

They give you just enough so you don't revolt. But never enough to stop depending.

Because true independence is dangerous.

If you had enough time to rest—truly rest—you might start questioning everything. If you had enough savings to walk away, you might. If you had enough confidence to unplug, they couldn't sell you back your self-worth.

The system can't allow that.

So it rewards your exhaustion with recognition. Your burnout with bonuses. Your quiet compliance with new titles. But not escape. Never escape. Just another level. Another ladder. Another goal.

And if you try to opt out? If you say, "I'm not playing anymore"? Watch what happens.

The support dries up. The praise evaporates. The compliments turn to confusion. You're no longer ambitious—you're lost. You're no longer focused—you're flaky. You're no longer winning —you're wasting potential.

The reward has been revoked.

Because you stepped outside the machine. And machines don't tolerate disruption.

Dependency is preserved by withholding enough to feel unfinished. You'll always be almost there. You'll always have "one more level."

Until one day you realize the goal was never yours. The goal was to keep you chasing.

REFLECTION QUESTIONS

- What parts of your daily routine are rooted in fear, not desire—and have you mistaken that for discipline?
- If your job disappeared tomorrow, what would collapse first—your income or your sense of identity?
- When you say you're being "smart" with money, are you actually being self-protective… or self-abandoning?
- How often do you accept 'just enough' because you're afraid of what might happen if you asked for more—or walked away?
- What's one system (financial, professional, social) you believe you "need"… but that actually drains you?
- Have you confused being busy with being free? Who benefits from you staying in motion?
- If you weren't afraid of being seen as a failure, what would you stop doing immediately—and what would you start?

CHAPTER SIX

WHEN SELF-WORTH HAS A PRICE TAG

"You didn't lose your self-worth. You sold it for applause."

BRANDED FROM BIRTH

You weren't born to chase status. You were taught to.

Before you ever learned how to write your name, you were being evaluated—graded, compared, measured. Not for who you were, but for how well you could perform. Not for your character, but for your usefulness. The branding didn't begin with logos or labels. It began with praise. With gold stars. With the clap of approval for sitting still, for coloring inside the lines, for being "good."

That's how early it starts.

A child draws on the wall and gets scolded. Not because it hurt anyone, but because it broke the rules. Another child cleans their room and gets rewarded. And in that moment, a silent lesson is planted: *Your value is conditional. It comes from pleasing others.*

That lesson blooms into a belief system. By the time you're ten, you've already linked love with performance. You know that when you get an "A," you're worthy. When you win the game, you're celebrated. When you impress, you belong. No one had to say it outright. The system made sure you absorbed it through a hundred little cues.

So you adapt.

You work harder. You learn to read faces before they speak. You chase applause without knowing you're doing it. You become fluent in the language of approval. You get addicted to the look in someone's eyes when you've done something right. And you carry that addiction straight into adulthood.

We don't call it addiction, though.

We call it ambition.

We call it being driven.

We call it "reaching your potential."

But here's what no one tells you: when your worth is outsourced from birth, your identity never really belongs to you.

It belongs to whoever holds the scoreboard.

Let's make it practical.

Why does a 6-year-old already know the difference between "smart" and "stupid"? Why does a 12-year-old feel ashamed if they can't afford brand-name shoes? Why does a teenager obsess over what job they'll have before they even know what peace feels like?

Because society doesn't wait for you to become someone. It slaps a price tag on your becoming—and tells you to earn it.

Education becomes the first auction block. Kids are rewarded not for curiosity, but for compliance. Creativity that doesn't translate into grades gets dismissed. Emotional intelligence goes unnoticed. The ones who fit the mold get ahead. The others get labeled.

The kid who memorizes fast? Gifted. The one who asks "why" too often? Disruptive. The student who copies well? Talented. The one who questions the lesson? A problem.

By high school, it's clear: those who master the system's logic—tests, rankings, rehearsed answers—are told they'll go far. The rest? They're quietly nudged toward "realistic expectations." Not based on capacity, but on conformity.

This isn't about school. This is about how you were programmed.

You didn't grow up asking, "What kind of human do I want to be?" You asked, "What kind of person do they need me to be… to matter?"

And that question haunts people their whole lives.

Because even when you escape the classroom, the grading never stops.

It just changes form.

Now it's job titles, social proof, follower counts, resumes, salary brackets, engagement rings. The metrics of self-worth just get more expensive. But the core message remains the same: *Who you are is only as valuable as what you produce—and what you earn for it.*

And the system keeps score relentlessly.

You're praised for being the first to arrive and the last to leave. You're respected for "staying busy," even if you're quietly dying inside. You're admired for your grind, even if you haven't rested in years. And if you slow down? People don't ask how you feel. They ask if you're okay financially.

Because in a world that worships doing, being becomes suspicious.

Let's bring this closer to home.

Have you ever introduced yourself at a party or networking event and said what you do instead of who you are?

That's not a fluke. That's branding.

You've been taught that your occupation is your identity. That your LinkedIn bio says more about you than your inner life. That your dating profile should list your career and fitness habits before your values.

And if you don't have the right "keywords" in that self-presentation? You're invisible. People swipe left on complexity. On slowness. On depth. Because the world isn't interested in your soul. It's interested in your utility.

The pressure to prove yourself starts early—and it never lets go.

You get your first job, and suddenly your output becomes a currency. You produce well, you get raises. You slow down, you get replaced. It doesn't matter how kind you are, how ethical, how emotionally attuned. If you don't produce, you don't matter.

And over time, that belief rots your insides.

Because when you're branded from birth, you start branding yourself.

You begin to think in packaging. You curate your online presence. You adjust your tone in emails.

You edit your vulnerability based on how "professional" it sounds.

You post, not because you want to, but because it signals "I'm still in the game."

You become a walking campaign. Selling yourself. Every damn day.

And calling it a career. Now here's the most painful part: the people around you reward it.

They applaud your discipline. They compliment your "drive." They post about you on social media as a "go-getter." And in that applause, you feel good for a moment. But it doesn't last. Because deep down, you know they're not cheering for you. They're cheering for your costume.

And the real you? The one underneath the performance? Hasn't been seen in years.

So you keep showing up in disguise. You keep branding yourself based on what sells. You dress for the part. You speak the language. You shape-shift into the version of you that will be approved.

You don't even lie. You just omit the parts that might make people uncomfortable. The parts that say, "I'm tired."

The parts that say, "I don't know who I am when I'm not producing." The parts that say, "I miss the kid I was before they turned me into a product."

This isn't just emotional decay. It's **identity fragmentation**.

You live in pieces. One for work. One for family. One for social media. One for yourself—buried beneath the others, half-forgotten, waiting for permission to come out.

And you've been so conditioned to equate worth with winning, that even your healing feels like a marketing campaign.

You meditate to perform better. You go to therapy to "level up." You do yoga not to reconnect—but to optimize.

Self-care becomes **another form of branding**. Another checkbox. Another performance.

Because you were never taught to exist without proving something. You were only ever taught how to **earn your place.**

But what if that was the lie? What if you were never meant to be productive to be valuable?

What if the real you is already enough—unbranded, unfiltered, unmonetized?

That idea feels uncomfortable. Even offensive. Because when you've been praised for your polish, it's hard to believe your rawness is still worthy.

But ask yourself this:

- When was the last time someone valued you without needing you?
- When was the last time you were celebrated for your presence—not your performance?
- When was the last time you sat in silence and didn't feel the urge to post about it? This is where the cost of the branding becomes clear.

You've spent your entire life being taught to trade authenticity for approval. You've learned how to be impressive.

But not how to be real. And now, even in your quiet moments, you judge yourself. You measure your worth by your output. You compare your timeline to strangers. You forget how to rest without guilt.

This is not your fault. It's the inheritance of a system that tagged you at birth. Not with love.

But with expectations. And until you name it, you'll keep living under its spell.

BECOMING THE PRODUCT

You were told to be authentic—but only if your authenticity could be packaged.

That's the modern trap. You don't sell a service. You don't sell a skill. You sell yourself. Your presence. Your style. Your personality. Your life. Your story. In today's economy, you are the brand—and your worth is measured by how convincing the performance is.

You were never given time to grow into who you are. You were taught how to perform who you needed to be.

That performance began small. You dressed a certain way to avoid being teased. You mimicked the tone of "successful" people in presentations. You softened your voice during interviews. You watched who got liked, who got retweeted, who got celebrated— and you adjusted accordingly.

And slowly, without realizing, you didn't just build a résumé. You built a persona.

It wasn't fake. That's what makes this harder to see. It was just edited. Sanded down. Optimized for appeal. You chose the versions of yourself that got results. You learned what to hide. You studied the algorithm of approval—and you played it like a game.

But it wasn't a game. It was your identity. And over time, the mask started to fit better than your own face.

This is how you became the product.

Let's talk about real life.

In today's job market, your résumé isn't just a document—it's your personal sales pitch. The average recruiter spends less than 10 seconds scanning it. That's how fast your worth is filtered. Not by your heart. Not by your growth. But by keywords, formatting, and performance metrics. You are reduced to your outputs before they even hear your voice.

And once you're in the job? The performance only intensifies.

Consider the experience of workers in client-facing roles—consultants, designers, even therapists. Increasingly, success in these roles depends not just on effectiveness, but on likability. Emotional labor becomes part of the product. You're expected to "bring positive energy," "be on brand," "stay professional"—even when you're exhausted or overwhelmed. Your emotional landscape isn't yours anymore. It's leased out for results.

Now take this same expectation and magnify it online.

Instagram, TikTok, YouTube—these platforms didn't just change how we communicate. They changed how we construct selfhood. A decade ago, people shared moments. Now they share personas. They curate "content" that aligns with their niche. They create aesthetics that signal identity—minimalist mom, self-help bro, nomadic entrepreneur, productivity queen.

But behind every feed is a person exhausted by curation. Trying to stay visible. Relevant. Marketable.

And the algorithm? It doesn't care about truth. It cares about engagement.

You perform yourself to maintain reach. You share the vulnerable story only when it can be captioned with a hook. You reveal pain only when it's paired with growth. You clean your apartment not for peace—but for a "reset routine" reel. You're not living for yourself. You're performing a self that looks alive.

Even ordinary people are expected to have a brand now.

A wedding isn't just a wedding—it's a content strategy. A vacation isn't a break—it's a background for lifestyle proof. Parenting becomes a portfolio. Friendships become stories. And slowly, even your offline life begins to serve your online narrative.

This isn't narcissism. It's the monetization of identity.

We reward those who perform their lives well. And we ignore those who don't.

Ask any creator who burned out trying to stay relevant. Ask any entrepreneur who lost their personal joy building a "personal brand." Ask anyone who built a following and then realized they can't say what they truly think—because they're trapped in the role their audience expects.

Even your pain becomes a product if you let it.

We now live in a world where vulnerability is valuable—but only if it fits a marketable arc. You can talk about your breakdown— but it has to end with a lesson. You can talk about your depression—but it has to end with a sunrise. You can talk about your trauma—but only if it fits into a carousel post.

This isn't healing. This is emotional packaging.

And here's the deeper pain: when you become the product, rejection hits differently. It's not your idea being critiqued. It's you. Not your work being ignored. You. The likes don't just reflect engagement. They reflect how visible your identity is allowed to be.

So you keep performing. Not because it feels right. But because not performing feels like disappearing. In this world, being seen is currency. So is being marketable.

Even in personal spaces—dating apps, social circles, networking events—the performance continues.

On Hinge or Tinder, you craft a profile that doesn't reflect your soul. It reflects your understanding of what others want. You highlight your job, your hobbies, your curated spontaneity. You add a joke, a prompt, a photo in nature. And you hope someone swipes not for who you are—but for how well you matched the performance of someone worth liking.

You weren't dishonest. But you weren't whole either.

You edited yourself—just like everyone else. Because being too real feels like a risk.

The same happens in friendships. You wear different emotional wardrobes for different people. You don't talk about money fears with friends who earn more. You hide your ambition around those who gave up. You mute your joy to avoid sounding boastful. You adjust. You filter. You perform.

Until one day, you realize no one knows the unedited version of you.

Not even you. This isn't about victimhood. It's about awareness.

You are not broken because you adapted. You adapted because you had to survive in a system that demands performance. But if you never take off the costume, you forget who you were before it was needed.

Let's talk about practicality again.

One of the most popular professional phrases today is "build your brand." Not your values. Not your boundaries. Not your craft. Your brand. That word now applies to people more than products. You're expected to "stand out," "own your niche," and "articulate your identity clearly." Why? Because in a hypercompetitive world, people need to know what you *represent* before they ever bother to ask who you are.

But this clarity comes at a cost: **dimensionality**. When you brand yourself, you flatten yourself.

You reduce your humanity into digestible traits. You become a category. You become someone's favorite flavor of content. And if you change? If you evolve? If you outgrow your niche?

You risk being abandoned by the very system that once applauded you.

That's the **paradox**: the moment you outgrow the version of yourself the world rewards, you become invisible again.

So you stay. You stay on-brand. You stay reliable. You stay legible. Even if it means silencing the part of you that wants to say, "I'm tired of this costume."

This system of self-performance is so normalized that we barely notice it anymore. We scroll through lives that look perfect and wonder why we feel so behind. We build identities that feel efficient but emotionally hollow. We lose the ability to distinguish between who we are and what we're performing.

Because the truth is: when you become the product, the line between authenticity and performance isn't just blurry. It disappears.

"When your worth has a price tag, you'll always feel discounted."

CURRENCY OF VALIDATION

Money was never just about survival. That's the lie you were sold to keep you docile. You weren't working just to live. You were working to matter.

Somewhere along the way, the number in your account became the number that defined your dignity. The price of your clothes became the price of your confidence. The digits on your payslip became the digits you used to measure your self-respect. You stopped asking "Am I enough?" and started asking "How much am I worth?"

That shift didn't happen overnight. It happened slowly, systemically—engineered over years of conditioning, capitalism, and comparison. You didn't even notice it. You just felt it. That quiet anxiety when you couldn't afford to split the bill. That shame when someone asked, "What do you do?" and you didn't know how to make it sound impressive. That deep, paralyzing embarrassment when your card declined and you felt like *you* were the one being rejected—not your balance.

This is the new architecture of identity:

money = merit.

It doesn't matter if you're kind, creative, loyal, or honest. If you're broke, you're invisible. If you're rich, you're right. You could be a terrible person, but if you pull up in a luxury car, the valet still opens your door with a smile. If you wear a tailored suit, no one questions your authority. You might be empty inside—but the world will still applaud your outfit.

That's the sickness.

Money isn't just a tool anymore. It's a mirror. And you've been trained to look into it to see who you are.

Let's get practical.

Look at how differently society treats a millionaire entrepreneur who declares bankruptcy versus a single mom who misses a rent payment. One gets a second chance. The other gets eviction papers. One gets a feature in Forbes titled "How I Bounced Back." The other gets labeled irresponsible.

The difference isn't the failure. It's the **perceived worth** behind it.

And that perception is shaped by money.

Ask yourself: how many times have you caught yourself justifying someone's opinion—just because they're wealthy?

You think, "He must know what he's talking about—look at his house."

"She's wearing a $900 blazer, she must be credible." "They run a million-dollar company; I should probably listen."

But wealth doesn't equal wisdom. Money doesn't come with morality. Yet we treat rich people like prophets and poor people like cautionary tales.

That's what happens when value becomes monetized.

Even self-help culture has been infected.

How many "gurus" are respected simply because they've made money off selling advice? How many people now measure their growth not by inner change, but by external results?

The modern path to "healing" often looks like this:

- Step 1: Burn out.
- Step 2: Quit job.
- Step 3: Post about "alignment."
- Step 4: Start a business.
- Step 5: Monetize your story.
- Step 6: Share screenshots of Stripe notifications.

And suddenly, your trauma becomes content. Your transformation becomes a funnel. Your inner work is now a personal brand —backed by receipts.

If you're not earning from your enlightenment, is it even real?

That's how warped the system has become.

It tells you: Your self-worth isn't something you feel. It's something you prove. And the proof? It better come in dollars.

But what if the money doesn't come?

What if the launch fails? What if the business never scales? What if the job market crashes again? What if you have a year of stillness, softness, slowness—and nothing to show for it?

That's when the real voice kicks in.

The one that says,

"You're falling behind."

"You're not enough."

"You should be doing more."

"You're wasting your potential."

That voice wasn't born inside you.

It was installed.

By systems that profit from your insecurity. By cultures that celebrate productivity over presence. By a world that has no use for your self-esteem unless it can be monetized.

It's why so many people tie their entire identity to a job title. Why being laid off feels like death. Why losing money feels like losing value. Because somewhere along the line, you stopped separating your net worth from your self-worth.

And now you don't know who you are without the paycheck.

Let's bring it closer.

Have you ever noticed how people speak differently when they talk about someone "successful"? They speak with more respect. More curiosity. Even if they don't like them. "He's a bit arrogant, but he's a genius." "She's intense, but she's built an empire." Translation: "They're rich. So whatever they're doing must be working."

Meanwhile, people who are struggling—no matter how principled, ethical, or insightful—get labeled as unmotivated. Lazy. "Nice, but they never figured it out."

We don't just judge outcomes. We judge worth—based on outcomes.

You see it in dating.

People filter based on income, ambition, lifestyle. Apps let you sort partners by education and career. And suddenly, people aren't people anymore. They're resumes. Brand partnerships. Vibes.

You see it in friendships.

Your value in the group chat rises if you "have your life together." You get invited more often when you're "thriving." People don't always say it—but they gravitate toward perceived success. It makes them feel secure by association.

You see it in your own behavior.

How you dress for the office versus how you dress at home. How you speak in meetings versus how you speak to your reflection. How you present your "wins" on social media—while quietly hiding the months you couldn't pay rent.

You might say you don't care about money. But the truth is, you care about what it symbolizes.

Respect. Belonging. Safety. Proof that you matter.

And that's the tragedy: we've turned money into meaning.

We use it to buy back dignity. We use it to demand love. We use it to silence shame. Not because we're greedy. But because we're desperate to feel whole.

But no amount of wealth can fix what dependency on validation breaks.

Because the moment your worth is outsourced, you're never allowed to rest. You're always chasing. Always refreshing. Always trying to do enough, earn enough, show enough—to finally feel like you're good enough.

That finish line doesn't exist.

Because the system profits from your pursuit, not your arrival.

So even when you hit your goals, the target moves.

You buy the car—and then you need the house. You get the raise —and then you want the title. You get the title—and then you need to prove you deserve it.

It's never-ending.

And the scariest part? If you try to step away from the race—if you say, "I want to be enough as I am"—you'll be told you're delusional.

People will say you've given up. That you're being irresponsible. That you're not playing the game right.

But the game was never yours. It was designed to keep you competing forever—for a sense of self you were born with but taught to forget.

And now, you're expected to buy it back.

"You didn't lose confidence – you outsourced it to your bank account."

THE IMAGE TRAP

Success used to mean security. Now, it means optics.

We no longer live to build real lives—we live to stage them. What we wear, what we drive, where we vacation, how we speak, even the books we leave on the coffee table—all of it is curated to signal something. Not who we are. But who we want people to believe we are.

In a world dominated by perception, image becomes currency. And once that happens, you stop making decisions based on what feels good or right or peaceful. You make them based on how they'll look to everyone else.

This is the image trap.

It's not about being shallow. It's about survival in a system that increasingly equates visibility with validity. The less people know who they are internally, the more they seek external signs to validate it. And in that vacuum, image rises to the top—not as an accessory, but as a requirement.

Let's get practical.

Think about the job market.

A person might be in massive debt, hate their field, feel emotionally drained, and lack any long-term joy—but if they wear the right blazer and carry a MacBook, they're seen as successful. Their apartment may be barely furnished, but the one room they film in is Instagrammable. The optics are clean, modern, upwardly mobile. No one asks what's behind the curtain. Because the curtain looks like achievement.

Now flip it.

A woman leaves a six-figure job to recover from burnout and live with less. She's healthier, happier, and more grounded than she's ever been. But she shops at thrift stores now. She rents a small apartment. She doesn't travel much. And suddenly, people worry. They assume she's fallen off. That something must be wrong. Why? Because her appearance no longer matches their idea of success.

This is how toxic the obsession with image has become. Freedom without presentation gets misread as failure.

The trap runs even deeper in social settings.

Weddings have become a performance of class positioning. Not just a celebration of love—but an unspoken competition. Destination locations, customized décor, branded hashtags, drones for aerial shots. Thousands spent—not for intimacy, but for the gallery. And couples justify it not because they want it, but because they fear being perceived as cheap, basic, or low-effort.

Birthday dinners become photoshoots. Vacations become backdrops. Relationships become aesthetic portfolios.

And if it's not posted, it didn't happen.

You see it in everyday decisions too.

People finance cars they can't afford—not for transportation, but for identity. Not because they need it, but because it says something. It completes a look. It elevates them above their current station, if only in perception.

Even how we work has changed.

Coworking spaces aren't just for convenience anymore—they're for visibility. A freelancer with a laptop in a high-end space appears more "legit" than one working from a kitchen table. The coffee shop with the right aesthetic has become the modern-day office. Not for productivity. For optics. For the feeling of playing a part in the script.

There's a word for this: **aesthetic inflation**.

The cost of appearing successful keeps rising. It's no longer enough to "have a job." You need a title that sounds powerful. It's not enough to relax. You need a curated "self-care" day. You can't just dress well—you have to look like a personal brand.

And that inflation is emotional too.

Every curated image creates pressure. If you post a luxury trip once, you're expected to "level up" next time. If your relationship looks perfect online, breaking up suddenly isn't just heartbreak— it's reputation damage. You don't just lose your partner. You lose the story.

People are now trapped in images they no longer relate to—but feel obligated to maintain.

And it doesn't stop with the rich. It happens across economic classes.

A man working a modest job spends a third of his paycheck on designer sneakers—not out of stupidity, but out of strategy. He's learned that in his social environment, appearance dictates respect. People listen to you more when you look "fresh." He might be exhausted, but at least he looks like he's got his act together.

He doesn't crave vanity. He craves dignity.

But when dignity is tied to image, freedom becomes unaffordable.

This is why so many people feel like they're suffocating inside lives that look good from the outside. They're stuck maintaining an identity that feeds the algorithm, pleases the crowd, and holds off judgment—but costs them their joy, honesty, and peace.

And the system encourages this.

It tells you to build a "personal brand." It turns style into strategy. It turns presence into packaging. It tells you that how you are seen is more important than who you are when no one's watching.

So you learn to pose in your own life.

You don't just cook a meal—you plate it for photos. You don't just rest—you record your rest as proof of balance. You don't just celebrate—you make sure there's content from it.

Even your healing becomes content.

You go on a wellness retreat and feel deep emotional release—but the moment is interrupted by the urge to film the sound bath. You finally slow down after years of burnout—but now you have to post about it with a long caption about "choosing alignment." You journal, but you think in tweetable lines. You meditate, but you're still half in Canva, planning your next quote card.

That's not healing. That's performance in disguise.

And the cost is subtle—but catastrophic.

You lose track of what's real. You start making choices not because they feel right—but because they look good. You skip the messy parts of life because they can't be packaged. You avoid conversations that don't photograph well. You sideline people who don't fit your online aesthetic.

And soon, your life isn't yours anymore.

It belongs to your audience.

This isn't just an influencer problem. It's a cultural epidemic. Even kids now are growing up thinking their value lies in how well they can present themselves. Teenagers are spending hours editing posts, worrying about engagement, measuring popularity in pixels. Middle-aged professionals feel pressure to prove their success through vacation pics and home renovations. Elders are sidelined if they can't adapt to the optics game.

The image trap doesn't care about your age. It only cares that you stay in it.

And here's the final irony: even people who look free are often the most bound.

That barefoot traveler who seems spontaneous? Check their credit card balance. That minimalist influencer? Check the sponsorship deals. That smiling couple in matching outfits? You'll never know how silent the dinner table was after the photo was taken.

Because curated happiness always hides something.

That's the real prison of the image trap.

You can't show the truth once you've built your worth on perception.

You can't afford to break the illusion.

You can't afford to be real.

But that's the invitation:

- What would happen if you dropped the performance?
- What if you let your house be messy?
- What if you didn't justify your slowness?

- What if you stopped editing your life for others?

You might lose applause.

You might get fewer likes. You might be misread.

But you'd be free.

Because the only thing more exhausting than trying to impress everyone… is living in fear of what happens when you stop.

REFLECTION QUESTIONS

- What part of your identity have you been performing for so long that you forgot who you were before it?
- If no one could see your job title, salary, appearance, or lifestyle—what would be left to define your worth?
- When did you first learn that "being impressive" got you more love than "being yourself"? And have you been chasing that ever since?
- What version of you are you afraid to show people— because it doesn't look "successful" enough?
- If you stripped away the need for approval, applause, and aesthetics—what kind of life would you actually choose to live?

CHAPTER SEVEN

THE INVISIBLE CHAINS

"You don't need bars to build a prison. You just need a clock and a paycheck."

THE CLOCK AS A COLLAR

Time used to be sacred.

It was measured in sunrises and seasons. It was marked by the sound of birds in the morning, by hunger, by fatigue, by the rhythm of life itself. You woke up with the world. You worked when there was light. You rested when the body asked. Time was personal. Internal. Yours.

But now? Time is a leash. A unit. A transaction. A countdown. Something you spend, sell, trade, and lose.

You no longer live by your own rhythm. You live by the calendar. By alarms. By time zones. By urgency.

Time is no longer just passing—it's being monetized.

And you? You've become a worker on the clock, not a person in the moment.

This didn't happen by accident. It was designed.

The system realized something very early on: if you can own a person's time, you can own their life. You don't have to control what they believe. You don't have to police their dreams. You just need to control when they wake up, when they eat, when they rest, and how much of their life is spent serving something outside of themselves.

That's how time became capital. And how you became a commodity.

Let's look at how it happened.

It started during the Industrial Revolution, when clocks moved from church towers into factories. Before that, most people—farmers, artisans, traders—worked in tune with the environment. But as mass production took over, time had to be measured, monitored, and managed.

Workers were no longer judged by their skill or creativity. They were judged by how many hours they could give. Time cards. Punch clocks. Hourly wages. The clock tower was no longer a public utility—it became a symbol of ownership.

Fast-forward to the present.

You wake up to an alarm set by your employer's expectations. You drink coffee not for pleasure but to beat fatigue faster. You sit in traffic, part of an army of bodies being moved according to someone else's schedule. You spend most of your waking hours doing tasks you didn't design, for goals you don't fully own, on timelines you didn't create.

Then, if you're lucky, you get a weekend.

But even that's not yours.

Weekends are for recovery. For errands. For laundry. For the meal prep you didn't have time to do because your weekday was already overbooked. And in the hours you *do* rest, there's guilt. Guilt that you're not using your time wisely. Guilt that you're "wasting" the only commodity that capitalism has taught you to value more than your body, your truth, your joy: productive time.

This is what ownership looks like when it's wrapped in convenience.

You clock in. You clock out. You earn your freedom one hour at a time.

But you never really feel free.

Let's go practical.

Ever looked at your calendar and felt dread—not because of the events, but because there was no room left to be yourself?

Meetings. Deadlines. Gym. Grocery runs. That "quick" coffee catch-up that drains an entire afternoon. You say yes because that's what adults do. You stay busy because you've been told that's what responsible people do.

But the more full your calendar gets, the more hollow you feel.

That's not a coincidence. That's architecture.

Modern systems are built on the assumption that **your time is a resource to be extracted**. That free time is wasted time. That empty time should be filled with apps, tasks, upgrades, opportunities.

Even your relaxation is scheduled. You go to yoga not because your body asked—but because your calendar had a gap. You book a weekend getaway but feel pressure to "make the most of it." You can't sit still without checking your phone—because stillness feels like laziness now.

Productivity culture has colonized your sense of rhythm.

And this isn't just about jobs. This is about life.

Schools train kids to sit in 45-minute blocks of focus. They stand in lines, ask for permission to speak, eat, leave. This isn't education—it's time conditioning. By the time they reach adulthood, they've already internalized that their day should be scheduled from morning to night.

It's no wonder most people can't enjoy an unstructured afternoon without guilt. It was trained out of them. Deliberately.

And the internet only made it worse.

Apps now measure how long you focus. Smartwatches tell you how well you've "optimized" your sleep. Calendars sync across devices, time zones, teams. And if you ever unplug? You fall behind. You get left out. You miss a ping. And in today's world, that's dangerous—because visibility is survival.

This is why you work through lunch. Why you answer emails at night. Why "five more minutes" turns into 90 on a Sunday afternoon.

Because you've been trained to believe that your time is never fully yours. That every unproductive minute is a missed opportunity to be more, earn more, achieve more.

Let's look at the corporate world.

You know what the phrase "billable hours" really means? It means your value is calculated by how many minutes you can charge someone else. It means your thinking, your presence, your availability—has a monetary value attached to the clock. No matter how good you are, your time has to be tracked to be validated.

The same applies to freelancers. Gig workers. Creators. No matter how "independent" you think you are, you're still on someone else's timeline. You're not judged by quality. You're judged by turnaround. Response time. Availability. Speed.

Speed has replaced depth. Presence has been sacrificed for productivity. Urgency has become the new intelligence.

You see it everywhere.

- People listen to podcasts on 1.5x speed.
- They buy 30-minute course summaries instead of full books.
- They take "power naps" designed to get them back to work faster.

Even rest has become a tool to get back to performing.

This isn't just time management. It's time extraction. And you're the one being drained.

Here's where it gets dangerous.

When you lose ownership of your time, you start losing ownership of your identity. Because time isn't just hours on a clock. Time is how you move through life. It's the soil where relationships grow, where art is born, where reflection happens. When your time is dictated by systems you didn't choose, your sense of self quietly evaporates.

You can't even answer "Who am I?" anymore—because your days are spent being what everyone else needs you to be.

You're a calendar.

A scheduler.

A responder.

A time slot.

And every now and then, when you feel overwhelmed, the world tells you to "take time for yourself." But that time? It's after the kids are asleep. After your inbox is cleared. After the bills are paid. After your nervous system has already gone numb.

That's not self-care. That's emotional triage.

This is why so many people feel like they're always running.

Always catching up.

Always behind on something.

Because they are.

Because the system was designed that way.

If you felt caught up, you might stop.

If you stopped, you might reflect.

If you reflected, you might realize none of this was ever about **you.**

And if you realized that? You'd become dangerous.

That's why control over your time is the deepest kind of control.

It looks soft.

It looks polite.

But it's a chokehold.

So what's the way out?

It starts with truth.

You have to admit that your relationship with time has been distorted.

That you don't need another planner, app, or productivity hack.

You need to reclaim your relationship with pace.

You need to remember how to feel time again. Not manage it. Not optimize it. Feel it. In your body. In your breath. In your bones.

It won't be easy.

Stillness will feel like failure at first.

Unscheduled hours will feel like risk.

But that's not your truth. That's your conditioning.

Because the truth is: time doesn't belong to them. It belongs to you.

Your mornings don't have to start with noise.

Your weekends don't have to be recovery from abuse. Your evenings don't have to be for catching up.

They can be for being. For living. For remembering what it's like to exist **off-script**.

You can't buy back stolen time. But you can stop giving it away.

And once you do, the system will notice.

Not because it cares about your healing.

But because it can no longer count on your exhaustion.

HIJACKED ASPIRATIONS

There's a quiet moment in everyone's life—somewhere between childhood and adulthood—when the question shifts from

> *"What do you want to be?"*
> to
> *"What will they let you become?"*

It's subtle. It's unspoken. But it's the exact moment when your dreams stop being yours and start being filtered through the system's approval.

We don't notice it when it happens. That's the danger.

Because by the time we're old enough to realize something was stolen, we've already learned how to thank the thief.

This is how aspirations get hijacked.

Not with force, but with reward. With rules. With promises. With systems that take your raw desire and dress it up in something marketable—something useful to the economy. And then they sell it back to you. Sanitized. Approved. Taxed. And now, no longer free.

Ask any five-year-old what they want to be, and you'll hear wonder. A marine biologist. A chef. A space explorer. A storyteller. A firefighter and a farmer at the same time. Their dreams are absurd, limitless, bursting with curiosity.

But something happens around the age of 10 or 12.

You start learning about "realistic goals." You're told which dreams make money, which are just hobbies, and which aren't "practical." You stop asking what excites you and start asking what's viable. And by high school, it's already hardwired: you pick a path that fits the mold, not your spirit.

That's the first layer of aspiration theft. It happens early. And it's wrapped in care.

Parents don't crush dreams maliciously—they're scared. The system scared them too. Teachers don't steer kids away from their passions because they don't believe in them. They're trying to protect them from a world that only rewards certain outputs.

And slowly, the pipeline begins.

School → University → Job → Mortgage → Retirement

Not because it suits your soul, but because it's the standardized template for "making it."

And the moment you veer from that script? You become "risky." You become "unfocused." You become someone who "needs to figure things out."

The irony? Most people *never* figured it out. They just got better at pretending.

Let's bring this down to Earth.

Look at the sheer number of people in careers they hate. Not because they're lazy. Not because they lack options. But because somewhere along the line, their dream was downgraded into a job description. The aspiring filmmaker becomes a digital content strategist. The poet becomes a copywriter. The child who once played doctor for the joy of healing becomes a surgeon who barely has time to sleep—let alone connect with patients.

Nowhere is this more visible than in the arts.

Take Viola Davis, for instance. A world-class, Oscar-winning actress who has spoken publicly about growing up in poverty and feeling invisible. Her original dream was not fame—it was *presence*. To be seen. To use her voice. And yet, even as one of the most respected actors alive, she has repeatedly said she still battles against a system that rewards her image more than her depth. That she has had to fight not just to act—but to be allowed to dream beyond the box Black women are placed in.

The system doesn't just hijack dreams. It assigns value to which ones are "respectable."

And if you want to chase a low-ranking dream, you better be prepared to justify it. To monetize it. To prove that it's not a waste of time.

That's what we've done to music. To writing. To athletics. To activism. Even love has to be "worth it."

Every dream must pass through the filter of ROI—Return on Investment.

Even tech entrepreneurs aren't spared.

Jack Dorsey, co-founder of Twitter, once said he was obsessed with maps, cities, and real-time systems. His original curiosity was about urban flow and communication networks. But somewhere along the way, that fascination became a platform—one he built, scaled, sold, and left behind. Despite his wealth, Dorsey often returns to minimalism and meditative silence. You can feel it in his later interviews: the rawness of someone who turned a dream into a machine, and then realized he missed the simplicity of why he started.

This is what aspiration hijacking looks like in real-time: You start with a fire.

The world turns it into a product.

And when the smoke clears, you don't recognize yourself anymore.

It's not always dramatic. Sometimes it's disguised as "doing what you love."

"Follow your passion," they say. But what they really mean is: *Follow your passion if it makes money. If it builds a platform. If it photographs well. If it trends.*

And if it doesn't? You're told to be realistic. To "pivot." To treat your passion like a side hustle—something cute, but not worthy of full-time energy unless it earns its keep.

Let's go even deeper.

Many of the dreams people carry aren't even theirs. They're inherited expectations dressed up as desires.

You become a doctor because your parents wanted security. You become a lawyer because it sounds powerful. You start a business because everyone around you is doing it.

You convince yourself you want it. You celebrate the milestones. But if you ever get still enough, you feel the disconnect. You feel the ghost of a dream you never gave yourself permission to pursue.

And now, you're too far in.

Too invested.

Too applauded.

So you keep going.

And the applause becomes a leash.

This is where the system's genius lies: it doesn't kill your dreams. It markets them back to you—with strings attached.

You wanted freedom? Here's a gig economy. You wanted art? Here's content. You wanted independence? Here's a startup, with 80-hour weeks and no boundaries. You wanted to travel? Here's a job that lets you work from anywhere—so you never stop working.

Even spirituality isn't spared.

You seek peace, and you're sold a $4,000 retreat. You seek healing, and you're sold a certification. You seek purpose, and you're sold a mastermind program.

The system doesn't care what you desire—as long as it can be commodified.

That's why so many people feel trapped even when they look successful. They got everything they wanted—except the *feeling* they were chasing. Because the system made sure the form was intact, but the soul was removed.

So what's the way out?

It starts with an audit.

Look at your current life and ask: *What part of this was my actual dream—and what part was just available, affordable, acceptable?*

Where did you shrink to be taken seriously? Where did you compromise without even realizing it? What part of you whispers in quiet moments, "I miss who I was becoming before this"?

These aren't small questions. They're seismic.

And they require you to face one painful truth: You can't always get your original dream back. But you can stop betraying the part of you that remembers it.

You can write again—even if it's not for a living. You can create —even if it never trends. You can heal—even if it makes no money. You can chase something slow, soft, unreasonable—and call that success.

Look at Rick Rubin, one of the most respected music producers in the world. He didn't build his empire by chasing what was popular. He followed stillness. He lived minimally. He produced from intuition. And his success came not from scaling—but from refusing to betray his sense of meaning.

Your dream doesn't have to die in the system. But it will need to be rescued from it.

And that rescue won't be glamorous.

It might look like letting go of something "almost right."

It might mean disappointing people who praised your ambition.

It might mean starting over—not with a plan, but with permission.

Permission to want what doesn't make sense. Permission to rest without apologizing. Permission to remember that your life is not a product.

Because the truth is: the system didn't hijack your dream.

It just offered you a cheaper version.

And you said yes because you were scared. Because you were tired. Because they made it sound reasonable.

But you don't have to stay there.

You can rewild your ambition. You can write new metrics. You can stop asking what's practical—and start asking what's *true*.

And once you do that, the system loses power. Because it can only sell you back your dream **if you forget it belonged to you in the first place**.

THE HUSTLE CAGE

Some prisons have bars. Others have calendars.

You don't need to be locked up to lose your freedom. Sometimes, all it takes is a to-do list, a packed schedule, and a story that says, *"This is what success looks like."*

Welcome to the hustle cage. It's invisible, self-imposed, and socially rewarded.

We've created a culture where busyness isn't just normalized—it's glorified. People wear it like armor. Like proof. If you're constantly tired, you must be doing something right. If you're booked solid, you must be important. If you have no time to rest, that must mean you're succeeding.

It's a lie that runs so deep, we call stillness laziness and exhaustion dedication.

Let's be real: most people don't want to be busy. They just don't want to look useless.

This didn't happen by chance. It's a byproduct of an economic system that needs you always in motion, always producing, always too tired to ask *why you're even doing any of it.*

And the most brilliant part? It convinces you that the hustle is your idea.

Take a look at the average working adult. They wake up to an alarm they resent. They scroll through emails before even brushing their teeth. They grab coffee—not for enjoyment, but as jet fuel. They jump into back-to-back meetings. They don't eat lunch so much as inhale it between tasks. And when the day ends, they don't unwind—they collapse.

This isn't life. It's a conveyor belt.

And if you dare to step off? If you say, "I need a break," or "I don't want to live like this anymore"—you're met with skepticism, judgment, even pity.

Because in a world addicted to performance, rest looks like failure.

Now let's bring in some reality.

Ariana Huffington, co-founder of *The Huffington Post*, collapsed from exhaustion in 2007, hitting her head on her desk and waking up in a pool of blood. At the time, she was seen as the picture of success. But behind the scenes, she was running on fumes. That moment forced her to confront a truth many ignore: the grind was not just unsustainable—it was erasing her.

She later built *Thrive Global*, a company focused on well-being. But the irony? Most people still admire her early hustle more than her current philosophy.

Because culturally, we reward burnout more than balance.

Look at the startup world.

Young founders brag about pulling all-nighters. Sleep becomes a weakness. The 4-Hour Workweek dream becomes a 100-hour reality. The office fridge is stocked with energy drinks. The Slack notifications never stop. Success isn't measured in peace—it's measured in how unavailable you are.

And when someone burns out, they're treated like a casualty of greatness. As if collapse is a rite of passage.

But collapse isn't a badge. It's a warning.

Take Simone Biles, the most decorated gymnast in history. In 2021, she withdrew from the Olympics to protect her mental health. She stepped back—not because she wasn't physically capable, but because she understood that her value wasn't just in how many gold medals she could win.

Her decision sparked global conversation. And it exposed a hard truth: even at the highest level, even after proving yourself over and over, the system will still expect you to sacrifice your wholeness for performance.

The cult of busyness doesn't care who you are. It only cares that you keep going.

Even in parenting, the pressure is real.

Mothers are told they must do it all—raise perfect kids, maintain careers, keep a spotless home, look great doing it. They schedule every moment: playdates, meal prep, homework checks, bedtime stories.

And if they take a break? They feel guilty. Like they're falling behind in some imaginary race.

It's not maternal instinct. It's hustle culture in disguise.

Even the concept of "me time" has been hijacked. It's now a slot between chores. A transaction. A buffer so you can be more productive later. Not a sacred pause—but a strategic pit stop.

The hustle cage is built with guilt.

It whispers, *"If you're not moving, you're wasting."* It teaches you to confuse rest with regression. It makes you feel behind—even when no one is chasing you.

You wake up with anxiety. You sleep with dread. You eat with urgency. You plan vacations with shame. You can't even enjoy Sunday afternoon without the looming shadow of Monday morning.

That feeling? The one where your body is still but your brain is sprinting? That's not productivity. That's panic, normalized.

Let's talk about how we glorify overwork.

> *"Grind now, shine later."*
> *"Sleep is for the weak."*
> *"I'll rest when I'm dead."*

These aren't just motivational slogans. They're battle cries of a system that treats people like machines. The problem? You're not a machine. You're not designed to run 24/7. And yet, the expectation persists.

Even leisure has become labor.

You can't read a book for fun—it has to be "on brand." You can't enjoy a walk—it has to close your rings. You can't take a nap—it has to be a "power nap." You can't even do nothing without justifying it as "self-care."

We've monetized peace. Packaged it. Put it on a productivity tracker.

And the result? A generation that is more connected, more efficient, and more exhausted than ever.

Let's be even more practical.

Why do people stay up late scrolling even when they're tired?

It's not stupidity. It's revenge bedtime procrastination—the only time they feel a sliver of freedom is at night, when no one is asking anything of them. When their time is finally their own. So they stay up—not because they're lazy, but because their life has been hijacked by duty. They're trying to steal back time they were never given permission to enjoy.

The hustle cage does that. It makes you grateful for crumbs of stillness.

And here's the most dangerous part: you start equating exhaustion with meaning.

You think, *"If I'm this tired, it must be worth it."* You convince yourself that stress is a sign of progress. You start measuring your days by output, not joy.

You've been taught to believe that rest must be earned. That joy must be delayed. That meaning must be mined from misery.

But what if none of that is true?

What if your worth isn't tied to how much you get done? What if your value doesn't increase when your calendar is full?

What if the most radical thing you could do… is *slow down*?

There's a reason billionaires now pay for silence retreats. There's a reason CEOs are learning to meditate. There's a reason even high performers are turning toward slowness.

Because deep down, they know: the hustle doesn't end in fulfillment. It ends in fracture.

Your body keeps score. Your relationships feel it. Your creativity dries up. Your spirit fades.

And eventually, the applause you chased so hard doesn't even matter—because you're too burned out to hear it.

So here's the truth:

You don't need another planner. You don't need to *"optimize your mornings."* You don't need to cram more into your already stuffed life.

You need to **exit the hustle cage**.

That might mean doing less. Saying no. Unsubscribing. Choosing slower work. Not answering messages immediately. Not chasing what looks good—but what feels honest.

And yes, people will judge you.

Because when you stop performing, you become a mirror. You reflect back everything they're trying to suppress. You remind them of the stillness they're scared to face.

But that's their burden. Not yours.

You were not born to be busy. You were born to be present.

And no system, no salary, no social pressure should have the power to take that away from you.

"They don't need to enslave you if you willingly trade freedom for a direct deposit."

MICROMANAGED SELVES

There's a moment far more dangerous than when someone controls you.

It's when you start controlling yourself in the way they trained you to.

That's when the system no longer needs surveillance cameras. It doesn't need managers. It doesn't need external enforcement. Because now, the voice of enforcement lives in your head. It lives in your planner, in your smartwatch, in your emails, in your guilt. It becomes internalized.

You don't rest because you're tired. You rest because you've "earned it." You don't work because you're passionate. You work because the silence makes you feel guilty.

This is the final trick of modern control: you become your own supervisor.

Let's be clear—this isn't personal weakness. It's the result of long-term, deliberate programming. Schools, workplaces, digital tools, and cultural norms all teach you that discipline equals morality. That productivity equals worth. And that if you're not constantly self-monitoring, you'll fall behind. Or worse, you'll become irrelevant.

This isn't efficiency. It's self-erasure.

Let's take a step back and look at how we got here.

It starts with performance-based reward systems from childhood. You get a gold star for good behavior, a sticker for perfect attendance, an award for following instructions. By the time you're in high school, your identity is tied to GPA, your future tied to standardized tests, and your weekends are filled not with exploration but with preparation.

You're not becoming a human—you're being shaped into a compliant worker.

Then come the productivity tools.

First it was to-do lists. Then it was planners. Then it was apps that buzzed, tracked, and gamified your life. You were told it was to help you focus. To improve. But what it really did was shift accountability away from systems—and onto individuals.

Now, if you fail, it's not because your job is exploitative. It's because *you didn't plan well.* It's not because you were overloaded. It's because *you didn't manage your time properly.*

The burden of burnout gets framed as a failure of personal discipline—not structural dysfunction.

This is where the idea of "micromanaged selfhood" begins. Not with a tyrant barking orders, but with apps that tell you to breathe. With devices that tell you how many steps you've taken. With calendars that track your life so precisely, you no longer know how to just *exist* without instruction.

And here's the part no one admits: a lot of us like it. We find comfort in structure. In control. In knowing that we're "on track."

But what if the track was never meant to lead to freedom? What if it was a treadmill, designed to keep us moving—without arriving?

Consider the rise of productivity cults.

You've seen them. The 5AM Club. The "No Zero Days" movement. Bullet journaling fanatics. People optimizing their sleep cycles down to 30-minute increments. None of this is inherently bad. But taken to extremes, it creates **internalized capitalism**: a state of being where your worth is measured by how little you rest and how much you optimize.

Even self-improvement becomes an industry of self-punishment.

You read books not for joy, but to "level up." You meditate, not to connect inwardly, but to improve performance. You track your meals, your workouts, your moods—not because you want health, but because you're terrified of failure.

You become both the master and the slave.

Let's make this real.

How many times have you relaxed and immediately felt like you should be doing something "more productive"?

That's not ambition. That's surveillance.

You've internalized the system's gaze. You don't need a boss hovering over you. You do it yourself. You open Slack at 9 PM just to "check in." You respond to emails on vacation. You apologize for delays even when you're allowed to be offline.

This isn't being responsible. This is being trained.

Real people feel this every day.

Take Sheryl Sandberg, former COO of Meta (Facebook). For years, she was praised as the gold standard of "doing it all"— mother, executive, author, Lean In icon. But even she admitted in interviews that she constantly felt the pressure to perform—to be available, composed, hyper-efficient. She internalized the need to appear perfect, even while advocating for balance.

The system doesn't care how powerful you are. It only cares that you keep performing—even if the stage is inside your own mind.

Even everyday tools reflect this.

The Apple Watch vibrates when you've been sitting too long. Your email has a red dot when you're "behind." Your calendar shows overlapping meetings—and you feel guilt for not solving the impossible. You're not just managing your life. You're managing perceptions of your efficiency.

And if you fail? You blame yourself.

But what if the system was never built to be humane?

What if the structure was always inhumane—and you've just learned to punish yourself before the system has to?

This is where micromanagement becomes self-discipline in its most toxic form.

It's not just about time. It's about identity.

You start believing that your most valuable self is the one that produces the most. That rest is dangerous. That spontaneity is suspicious. That joy must be justified.

Even hobbies become hustles.

You like painting? Open an Etsy shop. You write poetry? Start a Substack. You enjoy yoga? Get certified and monetize it.

The idea of doing something purely for yourself becomes so foreign that people feel guilty if they're not turning everything into content or commerce.

We are now a generation of people trying to heal… through the same systems that made us sick.

Even self-care has been weaponized.

You light candles, take a bath, and post it on Instagram with a quote about "taking time." But if it's not documented, it doesn't feel valid. If no one sees it, did it even count?

You become the marketing department for your own healing. And that's not recovery. That's branded exhaustion.

Let's talk about famous people who've escaped—or tried to.

Dave Chappelle, one of the most respected comedians alive, famously walked away from a $50 million deal with Comedy Central. Why? Because he saw the machine trying to twist his art into something he didn't believe in. In interviews, he's talked about how freedom wasn't about money—it was about time, integrity, and agency.

He didn't want to be micromanaged by ratings. He didn't want his identity shaped by executives. So he left. Not because he lacked discipline—but because he refused to perform a version of himself that didn't feel true.

That's what stepping out of the micromanaged self looks like. And it's terrifying.

Because once you stop self-surveilling, the world starts to panic.

People don't know what to do with someone who doesn't perform on cue. Someone who says no. Someone who disconnects. Someone who doesn't respond to urgency with obedience.

You become unpredictable. And unpredictable people are dangerous to systems built on routine.

But let's also be fair: some self-discipline is necessary. We do need structure. We do need accountability. We do need boundaries.

The problem is when structure becomes suffocation.

When discipline becomes self-harm. When tracking becomes obsession. When self-awareness becomes constant self-surveillance.

And here's the cost: you lose the ability to hear your intuition.

Because when you're always performing for your inner critic, your real voice—the one that says "this doesn't feel right"—gets drowned out.

You know the voice I'm talking about.

The one that whispers, *Slow down.* The one that says, *You don't have to prove anything.* The one that remembers who you were before all this.

That voice is still there. But you've taught yourself to ignore it. Because it's not efficient. Because it doesn't hustle. Because it doesn't care about algorithms.

But that voice is the key.

That's the part of you that hasn't been colonized. That's the part that still knows how to rest without guilt. That can do nothing and not feel empty. That doesn't need to be micromanaged—because it was never broken.

So how do you return to it?

Start by breaking the illusion of control.

Don't check your email first thing in the morning. Let a message go unanswered. Miss a deadline if it's killing your spirit. Choose peace over performance—even when no one's watching.

It will feel wrong at first. That's okay. That's detox. That's what it feels like when you stop being the system's agent inside your own head.

Because you were never meant to be a manager of yourself. You were meant to be a steward of your soul.

And there's a difference.

One measures. The other listens. One optimizes. The other honors. One punishes. The other forgives.

The micromanaged self believes worth is earned through exhaustion. The real you remembers that worth was never in question.

So drop the act.

Close the tab.

Step outside the cage.

You're not lazy. You're not undisciplined. You're tired of treating yourself like a machine.

And that's not failure. That's awakening.

HYPERCHOICE PARALYSIS

You were promised freedom. But what you got was the illusion of choice.

Modern life is saturated with options—every decision, from what to eat to how to work, is met with a barrage of alternatives. Apps to plan. Apps to optimize. Apps to outsource your brain. Thousands of courses. Dozens of productivity systems. Career paths with 15 sub-niches. Health advice from a hundred contradicting influencers.

You can shop at a grocery store with 187 kinds of bread. You can scroll through 14 dating apps and still feel lonely. You can open Netflix, browse 12 categories of entertainment… and end up watching nothing.

What you're experiencing isn't freedom. It's hyperchoice paralysis —a condition where too many choices stop you from choosing at all.

And it's not a glitch in the system. It's how the system maintains control.

Because when you're overwhelmed, you're easier to manipulate.

When you're unsure, you outsource decisions.

When you're constantly comparing, you forget how to feel.

You trade clarity for convenience—and you call it autonomy.

But choice isn't always power. In a world like this, choice becomes a distraction.

Let's go practical.

Imagine a 25-year-old deciding on a career. He's got a degree, maybe a few internships under his belt. What does he see when he opens his laptop?

- Start a startup.
- Go freelance.
- Be a content creator.
- Work at a tech company.
- Join a nonprofit.
- Learn to code.
- Move abroad.
- Launch a personal brand.

- Take a gap year.
- Go to grad school.
- Try five side hustles.

On paper, this looks like empowerment. But in his head? It's chaos.

He's not excited. He's paralyzed.

Because when every choice promises transformation, making the wrong one feels fatal. And when you're terrified of choosing wrong, you delay, scroll, panic, and start relying on other people's frameworks to make sense of your life.

And just like that, your choices aren't yours anymore.

They belong to algorithms, trends, influencers, mentors, and "10-step guides" that were never written for the life you want.

This is what hyperchoice does. It makes confusion feel like your fault, when really it was engineered by a system that profits from your indecision.

Look at how shopping has changed.

A generation ago, you walked into a store. You picked between two or three options. You left.

Today? You browse Amazon for hours. Hundreds of options. Filters. Reviews. Ratings. Delivery times. Sponsored suggestions. Fake reviews posing as helpful.

You don't feel like a shopper. You feel like a researcher—drowning in tabs and uncertainty.

And this doesn't make your life easier. It drains your cognitive energy. It introduces doubt where there was none. You were just trying to buy a toothbrush—and now you're having an existential crisis about bristle firmness and enamel protection.

This isn't freedom. This is a system that confuses abundance with agency.

And it gets worse when it comes to identity.

Go on social media and you'll find 300 "paths to success." Everyone's a coach. Everyone has a framework. Everyone is telling you that if you just follow their model, you'll unlock your potential.

But when you're inundated with blueprints, you stop building your own house.

You become addicted to guidance. You mistake clarity for safety. And soon, your entire sense of direction is based on which person yelled the loudest this week.

This is hyperchoice at its core: Too many options, too little self-trust.

Let's talk about dating.

Hyperchoice has turned connection into calculation. On dating apps, you can swipe through hundreds of people without saying a word. There's always someone else. Always a better match. Always another option.

You think this makes love more accessible. But it doesn't. It makes people disposable.

Because when you're constantly choosing, you're never committing. When you're always optimizing, you're never surrendering. You're not choosing someone—you're editing a spreadsheet.

And then you wonder why you feel alone.

The system tells you that with enough filters, enough criteria, enough effort, you'll find the "perfect fit." But perfection is the enemy of presence.

Hyperchoice kills intimacy—not because you don't want connection, but because you're trained to compare instead of commit.

It doesn't stop at relationships.

Look at fitness culture. Thousands of programs. Keto. Paleo. Vegan. Intermittent fasting. High-protein. Low-carb. CrossFit. Pilates. Strength training. Biohacking. Cold plunges. Hot yoga. Supplements. Fasting mimicking. Wearables. Tracking apps. Fitness watches.

You spend so much time researching the right plan, you never actually move your body.

You follow 12 fitness influencers with different philosophies and end up so mentally cluttered you do nothing. And when nothing works, you blame yourself. You think you lack discipline. But the truth is: you're just burnt out from deciding.

This is the real cost of hyperchoice: Decision fatigue becomes identity fatigue.

You don't just feel stuck. You feel like *you're the problem.*

But you're not.

The problem is that we were never designed for this many choices—especially not on demand, at speed, without pause.

You can't make meaningful decisions when your nervous system is constantly overwhelmed.

Let's look at how this plays out psychologically.

Psychologist Barry Schwartz coined the term **"The Paradox of Choice"**—the idea that too many options lead to anxiety, dissatisfaction, and paralysis.

His studies showed that when people had fewer choices, they were more likely to take action and be happy with their decision. But when faced with too many options, people second-guessed themselves, blamed themselves more, and experienced regret—even if they chose well.

And this doesn't just affect what you buy.

It affects how you shape your life.

Because the more choices you're given, the more you're taught that you're personally responsible for everything.

Not happy? That's your fault. You picked wrong. Burned out? You should've optimized better. Lonely? You swiped the wrong way. Broke? You didn't pick the right side hustle.

In a world of hyperchoice, freedom gets twisted into self-blame.

And when that blame piles up, you stop choosing altogether. You live in limbo. You scroll. You numb out. You stay stuck—not because you're lost, but because the map is so cluttered, you can't see the road.

This is why people get addicted to "life design" content but never actually design their life. Why they build mood boards instead of momentum. Why they change apps, mentors, or tools—but never change direction.

They're not lazy. They're over-available to possibility—but under-committed to clarity.

Let's bring in a real-world example.

Zuckerberg and Jobs both famously wore the same outfits every day. Not because they lacked style. But because they understood the cost of decision fatigue. Every choice you make burns mental energy. By eliminating small choices, they protected their focus.

Now apply that same principle to your own life.

How much of your exhaustion comes not from action—but from endless micro-decisions that drain your mental bandwidth?

From the moment you wake up, you're making decisions: What to wear. What to eat. What to watch. What to post. Who to reply to. Which project to start. Which idea to pursue.

Each one seems small. But collectively? They consume your attention like a leaking faucet.

And here's the irony: The more choices you have, the more you seek certainty.

That's why you binge watch productivity content. Why you download every life-planning template. Why you keep trying new systems instead of building momentum.

You don't want more tools. You want fewer distractions.

You want depth—not more tabs open.

So what's the way out?

It's not about reducing ambition. It's about reducing noise.

You need to reclaim deliberate constraint.

Deliberate constraint is the radical act of limiting your options on purpose, not because you're weak—but because you want your energy back.

It means:

Choosing one direction and letting others die without mourning them.

Saying "no" not just to what's bad—but to what's *almost good*.

Living by your values instead of your notifications.

Letting your boredom stretch long enough to hear your real desires underneath the clutter.

This isn't easy.

Because everything around you—every ad, every influencer, every app—is screaming, "More is better! More is freedom!"

But that's not freedom. That's capitalism disguised as empowerment.

Real freedom is not having every option. Real freedom is **knowing which ones you no longer need**.

"You're not stuck – you're sedated, silenced, and praised for playing along."

REFLECTION QUESTIONS

- When did your life stop feeling like a choice and start feeling like a checklist—and who benefits from that?
- What's one part of your day that feels automatic, draining, and unexamined—but you still do it out of guilt or fear?

- If no one were watching, tracking, or measuring you—how would your days look different?
- What dream or desire have you delayed not because it's impractical—but because you're overwhelmed by all the possible ways to pursue it?
- What is one small, quiet act of self-reclamation you could take this week to remember that your time, your dreams, and your identity are still yours?

CHAPTER EIGHT

BREAKING THE SPELL

"Addiction isn't about pleasure. It's about what you're afraid to feel without it."

WITHDRAWAL SYMPTOMS

Letting go of an addiction doesn't start with peace. It starts with panic. And when the addiction is money, the withdrawal isn't just emotional—it's existential. Most people believe that moving away from a money-centered life will bring calm, clarity, and simplicity. What they don't anticipate is the turbulence that comes first. Because the moment money stops being your compass, your system doesn't breathe a sigh of relief. It panics. The silence is louder than the noise ever was. You feel unanchored, not enlightened. That's not a failure of discipline—it's the expected collapse of a structure your self-worth was built on.

Money addiction rarely looks like greed. It looks like chronic productivity. It looks like guilt when you rest. It looks like tying your mood to your bank balance. When you begin detaching from this wiring—when you stop chasing promotions, downsizing your lifestyle, saying no to things that used to validate you—you start experiencing symptoms that feel eerily similar to drug withdrawal: mood swings, restlessness, irritability, even fear of worthlessness. Your nervous system isn't malfunctioning. It's recalibrating. You're not failing to live without money as your anchor. You're facing the detox your culture never warned you about.

This anxiety isn't abstract. It's practical. People often feel embarrassed when they can't enjoy their "freedom" after downsizing or slowing down. Someone quits a high-paying job to pursue a simpler life and suddenly finds themselves waking up with dread. Not because they miss their job, but because they don't know how to measure themselves anymore. Their productivity was their purpose. Now, without metrics, they feel invisible. This is a psychological crash, not a motivational dip. The brain, trained for years to associate success with speed and income, now has no reward signal to chase. And when there's no reward, the brain defaults to threat. That's why even minor expenses can feel stressful. That's why idle time feels unbearable. That's why silence feels unsafe.

There's also a collective layer to this withdrawal. Society continues to celebrate wealth even when it robs people of joy. High-profile entrepreneurs like Elon Musk work 100+ hour weeks and sleep on factory floors—not as a sign of imbalance, but as a badge of honor. Media presents these habits as admirable, aspirational. But beneath the surface is an entire class of high-performing individuals who are incapable of stopping—not because they love what they do, but because they're terrified of what stillness will reveal. Musk has openly stated that he finds it hard to be happy and often feels immense loneliness. The system might reward the grind, but it bankrupts the self.

When you begin your own detox—whether that means earning less, spending less, downsizing, or rejecting status signals—you may start feeling like you're disappearing. Friends who once admired your ambition may now seem confused by your choices. Social invitations might slow down. You'll begin noticing how much of your identity was propped up by how "useful" or "successful" you appeared. When you no longer lead conversations with your job title, people listen differently. When you're not upgrading your lifestyle, no one congratulates you. It's not just financial withdrawal—it's social invisibility. And it hurts.

What's even more destabilizing is that the culture doesn't give you a language for this pain. If you complain, you sound privileged. If you admit to struggling, people question your ambition. So you internalize the disorientation. You tell yourself you're just not trying hard enough. But that's the voice of your old addiction trying to pull you back in. Because the system doesn't need to punish you when it's already trained you to punish yourself.

The early stages of detox often bring irrational cravings. Not for money itself, but for the psychological props it offers. You'll miss the dopamine hit of checking your balance and seeing growth. You'll miss the rush of planning for upgrades. You'll miss the sense of forward momentum that comes with chasing more. These aren't desires—they're withdrawal spikes. They're echoes of a nervous system that only ever felt safe in motion. Letting them pass is part of the work. But expecting them is what makes the work survivable.

There's also grief in this process. Grief for the time you lost obsessing over "more." Grief for the relationships that were built on shared ambition, not shared values. Grief for the version of you that chased success not out of desire, but out of fear. The grieving isn't clean. It shows up in the strangest places. You may find yourself resenting people who are still chasing money, even if you were doing the same thing six months ago. You may feel jealousy toward others who appear happy in minimalism, while you secretly feel hollow. You may look at your bank account and feel both pride and shame simultaneously. These contradictions are part of the rupture.

Even people with immense wealth have reported this hollowing. In his memoir *Shoe Dog*, Nike founder Phil Knight admitted that building a billion-dollar empire didn't quiet the existential void. He described feeling lost, even haunted, after retirement. Money, he said, gave him control—but never peace. He was so addicted to movement, to pursuit, that once he reached the finish line, there was no identity left to inhabit. That's the final symptom of withdrawal: realizing that you don't miss the money. You miss the distraction it gave you from the truth of who you've become.

At a practical level, money withdrawal often triggers behavioral compulsions. You might overanalyze every purchase. You might obsess over spreadsheets that used to comfort you. You might try to "replace" money-chasing with something else—an identity shift, a new diet, an overcommitment to wellness or minimalism. Detoxing from money addiction doesn't just strip your financial habits—it exposes your avoidance mechanisms. What you grab for next is often what you used money to run from in the first place. That's the moment of truth. When the distraction falls, you meet yourself again.

But there is hope embedded in the pain. Withdrawal means your body is learning to operate without a dependency. It means your sense of safety is no longer tethered to something external. It means your nervous system is beginning to recognize stillness not as danger, but as home. This is where the rebuilding begins. Not when you're free of discomfort—but when you stop fleeing it.

Most systems don't teach people how to be free. They teach people how to comply and call it success. So when you stop complying, when you stop using money as your moral compass, don't expect immediate joy. Expect collapse. But let that collapse be sacred. Because beneath the rubble is the foundation you never built for yourself. A foundation not made of numbers or status—but of inner knowing.

Freedom isn't the absence of stress. It's the ability to sit with discomfort without bargaining your soul for relief. And if you can survive the silence that follows when the money drug begins to fade—what you'll hear next is the voice of a self you haven't met in years.

"If your peace collapses the moment you stop chasing money, it was never peace - it was sedation."

UNLEARNING VALUE

For most of your life, you were told what mattered.

You were taught to chase grades, then job titles, then income brackets. You were handed a script: work hard, earn well, build assets, accumulate status, and eventually, you'll arrive at something called a meaningful life.

But no one ever told you what meaning actually feels like. They only told you how it looks.

You believed meaning was external. That it came with applause. That it came from productivity, prestige, or praise. That it would arrive with a job offer, a promotion, a number in your bank account.

So you chased what they told you to chase. And if you're here now—detoxing, rethinking, unraveling—then chances are you've already tasted the aftermath: the confusion, the hollowness, the question that haunts the silence—

What actually makes this life worth living?

That's the hardest part of recovery from money addiction: realizing that your sense of value was never yours to begin with.

It was inherited. Trained. Rewarded. Sold to you through performance, convenience, and comparison.

Unlearning value doesn't mean becoming careless. It means confronting the truth that you've been performing meaning, not living it.

It means recognizing that chasing success was never about joy—it was about seeking proof.

Unlearning value means asking the question that rarely gets asked in ambition culture: *Who were you before they taught you what to want?*

And more importantly: *Can you remember what mattered to you before you were told it had to be profitable?*

This kind of unlearning isn't intellectual. It's emotional. It shakes the foundation of your decision-making. It disrupts how you relate to your time, your goals, your relationships.

Because once you realize you've been living by someone else's definition of worth, everything you've built starts to look unstable.

You begin to feel like a stranger in your own accomplishments.

Unlearning value often starts with disillusionment. You reach the thing you thought would fulfill you—and it doesn't. You get the job, and you feel nothing. You hit the savings goal, and you still don't sleep well. You move into the better apartment, but it doesn't make you feel more at home in yourself.

That's not entitlement. That's awakening.

That's the quiet grief of realizing you spent years climbing a ladder that was never leaning against a wall you cared about.

This isn't a crisis. It's a beginning.

The process of redefining value begins where the old metrics die.

It begins in silence, when you no longer have performance to hide behind. It begins in honesty, when you admit you don't know who you are without your calendar or your earnings or your title.

It's terrifying. But it's sacred.

And it leads to something deeper than success: alignment.

One of the clearest modern examples of this kind of unlearning is actor and humanitarian Angelina Jolie. At the height of her fame, she had everything the world defined as meaningful—beauty, wealth, global attention. But it wasn't until she began humanitarian work with the UNHCR that she described feeling *grounded* for the first time. She has spoken openly about how the experience of seeing displaced families and vulnerable communities changed her entire value system.

She didn't give up acting. She didn't renounce her career. But she stopped letting her **value** be measured by scripts and awards. She redefined meaning through service, empathy, and the quiet impact of showing up for people the world ignored.

That's unlearning.

It doesn't always require a dramatic pivot. Sometimes it just means choosing to care about things that don't scale.

The modern world doesn't celebrate that kind of shift. It doesn't know what to do with people who stop chasing visibility. It punishes stillness with irrelevance. It tells you that if your life can't be measured or monetized, it must not be meaningful.

But that's the old value system talking. The one that sold you busyness as purpose and wealth as wisdom.

The new one—*your* new one—has to be defined on different terms.

And that means going deeper.

Start with time. How much of your time is spent doing things that bring you back to yourself, rather than things that prove your worth?

It's a confronting question. Because for many people, the honest answer is: almost none.

We fill our schedules with obligations, goals, and optimizations. Even our rest is designed to make us "better."

But value isn't always visible. Some of the most meaningful moments are inefficient, unproductive, and unplanned.

Walking without your phone. Spending time with people who don't care what you do for a living. Cooking slowly. Reading for no reason. Helping without documenting. Sitting in grief without rushing it.

These aren't glamorous. But they're real. They're not metrics. They're moments. And meaning lives in moments—not milestones.

This is where practicality enters.

Redefining value doesn't mean living in a cave or rejecting money. It means consciously choosing what **you** want to center.

It means asking:

- If I weren't trying to impress anyone, what would I do today?
- If my success couldn't be posted online, how would I define it?
- If I had one year to live, what would become irrelevant? What would become sacred?

People who've faced mortality often answer these questions clearly.

When Apple co-founder Steve Jobs was diagnosed with cancer, he began publicly reflecting on the illusion of external success. In his Stanford commencement speech, he said, "Remembering that I'll be dead soon is the most important tool I've ever encountered to help me make the big choices in life... because almost every-thing—external expectations, pride, fear of embarrassment or failure—just falls away in the face of death, leaving only what is truly important."

For someone who helped shape the world's most profitable tech company, those words carry weight.

Because even Jobs, a titan of performance and innovation, recognized that value isn't in what you build. It's in what outlives your ego.

Redefining value means letting death teach you how to live.

It doesn't mean becoming reckless. It means becoming real.

Letting go of the script doesn't make you lost. It makes you free.

But freedom is uncomfortable at first. Because once you stop measuring your life in numbers, there's nothing left to compare it to.

And without comparison, you have to start feeling again.

You have to feel your values, not just recite them.

You have to sit with regret—not to punish yourself, but to learn what matters to you now.

You have to unlearn what the world told you was meaningful—so you can remember what it means to matter to yourself.

This isn't easy work.

But it's necessary if you want a life that doesn't collapse every time your income dips or your job changes or the applause stops.

Practicality lives in the quiet habits you adopt as new anchors.

It's in how you start your mornings—not to optimize the day, but to ground your presence.

It's in who you prioritize in your week—not based on convenience, but on connection.

It's in how you make financial decisions—not based on scarcity or status, but based on sustainability and self-respect.

Value becomes personal again. Private again. Real again.

It's not a brand. It's not a performance. It's not a bullet point.

It's how you feel in your body when you stop pretending.

If your worth depends on what you produce, then who are you when you're not performing?

LEARNING TO SIT WITH EMPTINESS

When people think about detoxing from money addiction, they imagine less spending, simpler living, fewer transactions. What they don't prepare for is the silence that follows. The absence. The space money used to occupy—not just in their bank account, but in their mind, their routine, their identity. It's in that space that the real test begins. Because it's not the absence of wealth that breaks you. It's the confrontation with what it was keeping at bay.

Money, for many, isn't about materialism. It's about management. It's how we manage boredom. Pain. Anxiety. Loneliness. Insecurity. The money chase gives you a script. It fills your day with tasks, your mind with goals, your time with purpose. Strip that away, and what's left? A quiet room. A slow morning. An afternoon with no direction. The hum of your own thoughts. For those who have built their entire self around movement and monetary milestones, that stillness isn't soothing—it's suffocating.

The truth is, most people aren't addicted to buying. They're addicted to distraction. Money is just the delivery mechanism. And the moment they stop using it as a shield, they start encountering emotional terrain they've spent years avoiding. They're not scared of being broke. They're scared of being *with themselves*—

without the buffer of productivity, without the thrill of acquisition, without the permission of a price tag.

Sitting with emptiness requires a level of emotional sobriety that our culture doesn't teach. From an early age, we're shown that feelings of discomfort must be fixed, outsourced, solved, or escaped. No one tells you that the discomfort itself might be the teacher. That what you feel in the absence of stimulation is not a sign of deficiency—it's a mirror.

Take former monk and mindfulness teacher Jay Shetty. He often shares how, after years in a London corporate job, he left to live in ashrams and train in meditation. What surprised him most wasn't the silence of the monastery—it was the chaos that emerged *within* when he no longer had the daily noise of achievement to hide behind. He described how the stillness forced him to meet himself in ways he'd never experienced. No applause. No deadlines. No career milestones. Just his thoughts. His fears. His impulses. That confrontation, he says, was more difficult than any corporate hustle he had ever endured.

Most people won't move to a monastery. But the principle is universal: when you strip away the scaffolding of financial performance, the scaffolding of self-image begins to tremble. You're forced to ask: *Who am I when there's nothing to prove?*

For some, that question triggers a spiral. In the absence of goals and gains, people reach for substitutes. They over-schedule. They over-clean. They over-consume under the disguise of minimalism. They swap shopping for biohacking. Capitalism doesn't care what you chase—as long as you don't pause long enough to ask why you're chasing anything at all.

The emptiness money used to fill is not empty by nature. It is simply unoccupied. And like any unoccupied space, it invites return. The return of sensations long buried: grief that was never processed, aspirations that were silenced, desires that were edited to fit into the market's mold.

This isn't abstract. It's bodily.

When you stop spending to escape, your nervous system doesn't relax—it flares up. You experience unease. Not because you're making the wrong choice, but because you've interrupted the loop. The dopamine cycle tied to consumption gets disrupted. And the brain, used to rewards, starts to panic in the presence of pause.

This is where the work begins—not with budgeting, but with breathing.

You have to learn to tolerate stillness. To sit in an afternoon without checking your account. To spend a morning in idleness without converting it into a "rest day" narrative. To go hours without optimizing your identity through posts, purchases, or productivity.

It's not about doing nothing. It's about allowing yourself to feel the weight of nothingness—and realizing it won't crush you.

Public figures who've chosen to walk away from noise often report this same pattern. Take J.K. Rowling, who disappeared from the public eye for extended periods after her initial rise to fame. She's spoken about the emotional toll of attaching self-worth to external validation and how, after the peak of her success, she intentionally stepped back—not to retire, but to detox. She described how sitting in quiet, without publishing or performing, forced her to separate her identity from her achievements. And it was in that stillness that her creativity began to resurface—not as obligation, but as exploration.

Rowling had wealth and fame. But what she lacked for a time was intimacy with herself. And she had to re-learn how to sit with that version of herself that wasn't adored, booked, or busy.

What's striking is how many people fear they'll lose their edge if they stop moving. That stillness will make them soft. That pause equals regression. But it's often in the pause that people remember what they were actually running from.

A client-facing professional may realize she never enjoyed her job —she enjoyed the adrenaline. A startup founder might notice that building companies gave him an identity when he didn't know how to build inner stability. A high-achiever might recognize that success wasn't a goal—it was a way to avoid abandonment. These truths don't emerge in motion. They emerge in emptiness.

There's a practice in Zen called "just sitting" (shikantaza). You don't chase thoughts. You don't solve problems. You just sit. And in that space, the mind reveals what the ego has hidden. You begin to hear what money drowned out: the unspoken fears, the suppressed grief, the buried joy. That kind of sitting isn't rest. It's revelation.

Learning to sit with emptiness also means learning not to fill it prematurely.

It's easy to swap one drug for another. You stop chasing money and start chasing "wellness." You replace business books with spiritual ones. You turn your slow living into a lifestyle aesthetic. But if you're still using those tools to numb your unease, then the addiction hasn't ended—it's just changed clothes.

The challenge is to sit with the discomfort without dressing it up. Without explaining it away. Without monetizing it or spiritualizing it. To let the silence remain awkward. To let your self-worth wobble without racing to reinforce it.

This is not laziness. This is labor. Inner labor. And most people will avoid it until something collapses.

Steve Wozniak, Apple's co-founder, once stepped away from the tech scene entirely. While Jobs was building the empire, Wozniak took a different path. He became a schoolteacher. Quietly. Privately. No media spectacle. No legacy optimization. Just a return to curiosity and contribution on his own terms. He walked away not because he had to—but because he didn't want to be trapped in an image. That decision wasn't passive. It was defiant.

He sat in the space others feared—the space without scale, headlines, or valuation. And in doing so, he proved that meaning doesn't have to be loud to be legitimate.

So what does this look like for you?

It might look like turning your phone off for half a day. Not to "reset," but to sit. It might look like leaving your finances untouched for a week—not because you're neglectful, but because you're detoxing from compulsive checking. It might look like spending time in a room without a screen or a goal. To let boredom in. To let unease visit.

These moments feel hollow at first. But they are hollow in the way a container is hollow—*meant to be filled with something real.*

What most people discover when they sit with emptiness long enough is that it doesn't stay empty. Once the compulsions quiet, something else emerges: softness, memory, intuition, insight. Not all at once. Not on command. But gradually, like a muscle rebuilding.

This is what makes the detox worth it. Not the minimalism. Not the frugality. Not the lifestyle shift.

The return to self.

When you no longer need money to shield you from silence, you become someone the system can't control. Because now your life is not built on noise—it's built on knowing.

And that kind of knowing doesn't chase worth. It sits with it.

Quietly.

Patiently.

Unapologetically.

If silence makes you anxious, it's not because something's wrong —it's because you've never heard yourself without the noise.

FINANCIAL CELIBACY

What happens when you stop earning on purpose?

Not because you lost your job. Not because you're burned out. But because you choose to pause. To reset. To detox your nervous system from the constant compulsion to monetize your existence.

That's what financial celibacy is. Not a budgeting tactic. Not a spiritual metaphor. A real, deliberate decision to stop using money to define your identity, your worth, and your safety. To voluntarily cut the cycle. To look money in the face, thank it for its role, and then walk away from the transaction—not forever, but long enough to know who you are without it.

It's not easy. In fact, it may be the most violent confrontation with yourself you'll ever have.

Because money doesn't just pay your bills. It pacifies your fears. It gives structure to your hours. It gives you something to chase when you don't know what else to live for.

So when you stop earning—even temporarily—you don't just lose income.

You lose the illusion of certainty.

You lose your role in the script.

You lose the scaffolding that made you feel valuable in a world obsessed with output.

And what's left is not peace. Not immediately. What's left is withdrawal. Dread. Boredom. Panic. You walk through your day not knowing how to measure your worth without checking a balance, sending an invoice, or closing a deal.

Financial celibacy is the cold turkey of capital. You don't wean off. You sever the tie. And in doing so, you discover how deep the dependency actually was.

For most people, money is not just a tool. It's a behavioral drug. It activates the reward center. It structures your choices. It becomes a form of dopamine regulation. You wake up for it. You sacrifice for it. You fantasize about it. You build entire lifestyles around it.

So choosing to step away—to stop earning, spending, upgrading, and optimizing—isn't just inconvenient. It feels like *death*.

Because part of you does die. The part that was engineered to be validated by capitalism.

This isn't theory. It's real. People have done it. And it broke them before it freed them.

Take actor Daniel Day-Lewis. After his third Oscar win, he left Hollywood—not in burnout, but in protest of what the industry demanded from him. He moved to Florence to learn shoemaking. Quiet. Anonymous. Non-performing. Not profitable. When asked why, he said he needed to step away to remember who he was without applause. He didn't retire to relax. He retreated to reclaim.

That's financial celibacy: reclaiming your sense of self from the grip of the system that commodified it.

This isn't about poverty. Or rejection of material stability. It's about the radical act of non-participation. Saying: *I will not define myself through profit for a while. I will not chase, upgrade, or accumulate. I will live within what I already have—and face the silence that follows.*

Because in that silence, the truth gets loud.

You realize how much of your personality was built to survive capitalism.

The hustle. The "I'm just wired this way." The pride in busyness. The obsession with progress. The belief that rest has to be earned.

These aren't natural. They're trained. And when you stop engaging in the financial treadmill, they surface like ghosts—begging to be believed again.

You have to sit with the part of you that doesn't know how to feel valuable without output. The part that looks at a slow afternoon and panics. The part that interprets non-earning as falling behind, rather than reclaiming sovereignty.

Most people never do this. They're terrified of what might surface.

Because the minute you stop earning, you're forced to confront a question that most people spend their entire lives avoiding:

What do I offer the world when I'm not for sale?

Not what can you sell.

Not what can you monetize.

But what remains when the price tags are gone.

That's where most people break. Not because they're shallow, but because they've never had to face that question without capitalism offering a pre-packaged answer.

- Your job title.
- Your productivity.
- Your ambition.
- Your lifestyle.

These are proxies for selfhood. And without them, you're left staring at the terrifying blank page of *you*.

Financial celibacy hands you that page. And doesn't let you look away.

Let's be clear—this isn't romantic minimalism. It's not a curated retreat. It's not about selling your stuff and moving to Bali. It's not "quiet quitting" with pretty photos.

It's about staying right where you are—in the mess, the mortgage, the city noise—and choosing not to participate in the rat race *any more than you absolutely must*. No new side hustles. No networking for future returns. No monetizing hobbies under the label of passion.

It's about letting your nervous system return to factory settings.

You stop listening to podcasts designed to get you rich. You stop reading "productivity hacks" and calling it growth. You stop watching others ascend and assuming they're winning.

You don't need a financial breakthrough. You need a break.

A break from the loop that says you only exist when you're useful.

That's what celibacy does. It teaches you to sit with the ache. The pause. The hunger for validation. And to not feed it with more performance.

For people who've never taken a break from earning, this can feel like a freefall. And the people around you won't always understand. You'll be told you're wasting time. That you're sabotaging your momentum. That you're not being realistic.

But what they're really saying is: *Your withdrawal is making me question my own addiction.*

Because financial celibacy is infectious. It holds up a mirror. It forces others to wonder what they're working for. Why they never stop. What they're really afraid of if they do.

People don't hate your pause. They hate what it says about their own pace.

That's why this path is lonely. There's no applause for non-performance. No medals for slowing down. The rewards are invisible—but they are immense.

You begin to sleep better. You begin to hear your thoughts without flinching. You begin to notice beauty you used to rush past. You begin to remember hobbies that didn't need hashtags. You begin to feel human again—not a project.

And then something even more unexpected happens.

You start realizing you never needed as much as you thought. Not just financially. But emotionally. All the craving for more starts to fade—not because you've given up, but because you've recalibrated your nervous system to want less and feel more.

You stop equating busyness with purpose. You stop justifying your rest. You stop chasing what never felt right to begin with.

And in that stillness, a new kind of clarity arrives. You see what matters. Not intellectually—but viscerally.

Relationships that feel nourishing. Work that feels aligned. Time that feels lived.

This doesn't mean you'll never earn again. It doesn't mean you'll renounce ambition. It means the next time you earn, it won't be to fill a hole. It will be from a foundation that's already full.

That's the power of financial celibacy. It removes the noise. It restores the signal.

You stop being seduced by scale. You stop performing for perception. You stop needing to explain your choices to people still trapped in the matrix.

And maybe, most importantly, you realize this:

You are not your productivity.

You are not your revenue.

You are not your potential to produce.

You are still here, even when you stop selling yourself.

And that, in this world, is the most radical act of all.

LIVING BEYOND METRICS

Enough isn't a number. It's a decision.

And that's what makes it so difficult to hold. In a world that trains you to measure everything—success, happiness, worth, growth—declaring that what you have, what you are, is already enough feels radical. Even dangerous.

Because once you stop measuring, you become unpredictable. And the system hates what it cannot calculate.

Practicing enoughness is not a self-help affirmation. It's not a gratitude list. It's not about settling or shrinking. It's the art of choosing satisfaction in a culture built on engineered dissatisfaction. It is psychological resistance. Economic rebellion. Spiritual defiance.

To practice enoughness is to withdraw your consent from the algorithm that says: not yet, not quite, almost there, just a little more.

And it's hard. Because you've been told since childhood that more equals better. That growth equals progress. That anything stable is stagnation. That staying still means falling behind.

You were never taught to recognize "enough." You were taught to fear it. Because if you ever felt satisfied, you might stop buying. You might stop striving.

You might stop obeying.

So they made you afraid of peace.

They told you it was laziness.

They told you it was failure in disguise.

The result? A generation of exhausted high-achievers, constantly moving, constantly comparing, constantly updating their goals, yet secretly unable to enjoy a single win.

Enoughness isn't natural to us—not because we're broken, but because we were groomed to keep wanting.

Look at how we've constructed progress. Economic growth is celebrated only when it's constant. A company's success is measured in quarterly gains. Countries aren't considered healthy unless their GDP rises. There is no metric for *sufficiency*. No celebration of "we have enough."

That mindset seeps into individual lives. You don't ask, "Is this sustainable?" You ask, "What's next?" You don't ask, "Do I feel peaceful?" You ask, "Am I maximizing?"

Practicing enoughness asks a different question: *What if this is already it?*

That question can be terrifying. Because if this is it, then you have to stop outsourcing your happiness to a future that may never come. You have to stop blaming your dissatisfaction on "not being there yet." You have to look at your current life—not as a stepping stone, but as the destination.

And that's where the discomfort lives. Because if your current life doesn't feel like enough, the question isn't what you lack. It's *why you thought more would fix it.*

This is not theory. It's visible in the most public lives.

Take fashion designer Vivienne Westwood, who built a global empire but lived modestly and consistently advocated for buying less. Her philosophy—"Buy less, choose well, make it last"—wasn't a marketing campaign. It was a rejection of consumption as identity. She practiced enoughness not as aesthetic minimalism, but as political intent. In interviews, she spoke with frustration about how excess had become the cultural norm, and how that excess was hollowing people out.

She wasn't anti-style. She was anti-endless hunger.

Enoughness doesn't mean you stop growing. It means your growth is no longer desperate. No longer tied to validation. No longer feeding an emptiness that was never meant to be solved with success.

Most people don't realize how addicted they are to metrics until they try to stop.

Stop tracking your steps. Stop checking your analytics. Stop counting the books you've read or the hours you've meditated or the habits you've stacked. What happens next isn't liberation—it's withdrawal.

Because your identity wasn't built on presence. It was built on progress.

You were taught to prove. To optimize. To quantify.

Enoughness asks you to quit all that.

To live a day without proving anything.

To move without tracking.

To love without performance.

To rest without permission.

And most people can't. Not at first.

Because enoughness strips you of your costume. It makes you face the naked reality of your life and asks, *Would you choose this even if no one clapped for it?*

And if the answer is no—then chasing more won't fix it. It'll just dress it up.

Enoughness begins with inventory. Not of your possessions. Of your patterns.

Where do you say yes because you're afraid of missing out?

Where do you keep upgrading because stillness feels unsafe?

Where do you pursue more not out of joy, but out of fear?

These aren't just questions. They're instructions.

Because the moment you identify the fear, you begin to see the game.

And once you see it, you can opt out.

That's what actor Keanu Reeves embodies so powerfully. In an industry built on hyper-visibility, Reeves lives almost anonymously. No social media. No performance of wealth. No racing toward relevance. He gives generously, lives simply, and protects his privacy like it's sacred. Not because he's hiding—but because he knows that value isn't determined by volume.

He's not competing. He's choosing.

And that's the secret to enoughness. It's not passive. It's powerful. You don't stumble into it. You *decide*.

You say, "This life—right now—is enough. Not perfect. Not static. But whole. And I will stop punishing it for not looking like someone else's highlight reel."

That kind of peace is dangerous. Because it breaks the cycle. It stops the scroll. It ends the chase.

When you practice enoughness, you begin to notice how often you were living in the *future*. You were waiting to be happy until you earned it. Until you got the offer. Until you bought the thing. Until you hit the goal.

And every time you got there, the line moved.

That's not failure. That's design.

Because as long as you're always almost enough, you'll stay in the game.

Enoughness is your exit strategy.

But it takes practice. Daily. Relentless. Compassionate.

Because the world won't stop seducing you. It won't stop whispering, *Just one more thing. One more course. One more follower. One more upgrade.*

You have to be louder.

Not with noise. With presence.

Wake up without checking. Move without tracking. Work without comparison. Connect without curating.

That's enoughness in motion. And it's uncomfortable at first.

Because it exposes the voids. The emptiness. The sadness you tried to outrun. But it also exposes the peace you were too busy to feel. The beauty that was always in the room. The love that didn't need approval. The joy that wasn't loud, but loyal.

Practicing enoughness doesn't mean you stop dreaming. It means your dreams are no longer bandages for unhealed wounds.

It means your goals serve you—not the other way around.

It means you can still build, still grow, still stretch—but from full-ness, not from fracture.

Enoughness is the foundation. Everything else is optional.

"They sold you a role in someone else's economy – now it's time to rewrite the script."

REFLECTION QUESTIONS

- What have you been using money to avoid feeling—and are you ready to sit with it instead of sedating it?
- If your income suddenly stopped today, who would you be without your job title, output, or role? Would you still recognize yourself?
- Where in your life have you confused growth with healing, progress with peace, or metrics with meaning?
- What's one area of your life you've never labeled "enough"—and what would change if you finally did?
- Are you living a life that actually feels valuable to you—or one that only looks valuable from the outside?

CONCLUSION

This was never just about money.

It was about what money replaced.

Silence. Stillness. Safety. Meaning. Worth.

You were sold currency as a cure. Value as a transaction. Identity as a balance sheet. You were told the more you had, the more you were. And you believed it. We all did.

Because the drug was everywhere.

It was in your classroom, your calendar, your coffee-fueled mornings. It was in the praise you got for hustling. In the shame you carried when you couldn't afford something. In the anxiety that crept in every time your value wasn't externally validated. In the high of the bonus. The low of the bill. The endless, choking loop of "not yet."

And now here you are—at the edge of withdrawal.

Raw. Awake. A little bit angry. A lot unanchored.

That's good.

Because you should be furious at what was done to you. You should be uncomfortable sitting in a system that taught you to monetize your time, your voice, your dreams, your self. You should question everything that made you think your life only mattered if it could be tracked, optimized, or sold.

This isn't about living with less. It's about dismantling the lie that more was ever the goal.

What happens now is up to you. No one's coming to hand you a new script. There is no seven-step plan to recover from being raised by capitalism. No course to help you feel safe in stillness. No investment portfolio that buys you back your soul.

The detox doesn't end. It deepens.

Because every day you'll be tempted. To chase. To scale. To prove.

And every day, you'll have to remember: what they sold you was a story. Not a truth.

You don't need another tool. You need to stop letting yourself be used.

They wanted you asleep. Productive. Polite. Predictable. But now, you're awake.

And no system can seduce someone who has seen it naked. Money is not evil. But addiction to it is. Not because it empties your wallet— but because it empties your life. So walk forward.

Not as a brand. Not as a commodity. Not as a cog. But as someone who knows what it cost to finally feel whole. And refuses to ever sell themselves again.

www.ingramcontent.com/pod-product-compliance
Lightning Source LLC
Chambersburg PA
CBHW061745120626
46550CB00005B/1898